FAITHFUL LEARNING

and the

CHRISTIAN SCHOLARLY VOCATION

Edited by

Douglas V. Henry and Bob R. Agee

William B. Eerdmans Publishing Company
Grand Rapids, Michigan / Cambridge, U.K.

D0686012

© 2003 Wm. B. Eerdmans Publishing Co.
All rights reserved

Wm. B. Eerdmans Publishing Co.
255 Jefferson Ave. S.E., Grand Rapids, Michigan 49503 /
P.O. Box 163, Cambridge CB3 9PU U.K.

Printed in the United States of America

08 07 06 05 04 03   7 6 5 4 3 2 1

Library of Congress Cataloging-in-Publication Data

Faithful learning and the Christian scholarly vocation / edited by Douglas V. Henry
    and Bob R. Agee.
        p.   cm.
    Includes bibliographical references.
    ISBN 0-8028-1398-4 (pbk.: alk. paper)
    1. Church and college.   2. Learning and scholarship — Religious aspects —
    Christianity. 3. Education (Christian theology)   I. Henry, Douglas V.
    II. Agee, Bob R.

    LC383.F35   2003
    378′.071 — dc21

                                                                2003049054

www.eerdmans.com

FAITHFUL LEARNING

and the

CHRISTIAN SCHOLARLY VOCATION

Contents

CONTENTS

PART TWO: CHALLENGES AND OPPORTUNITIES

Acknowledgments

We offer grateful appreciation to many who helped bring this book to birth. We are grateful to all of the contributing authors, for their diligence in first preparing illuminating talks for the annual H. I. Hester Lecture Series, for adapting their lectures for publication in the quarterly *Southern Baptist Educator,* and for their willingness more recently to revise and update the material for the purposes of this collection. The lecture series is held each year in conjunction with the meeting of the Association of Southern Baptist Colleges and Schools (ASBCS). Hubert Inman Hester, longtime professor and administrator at William Jewell College, endowed the lecture series in 1971 with the desire that it advance understanding of the aims, challenges, and opportunities of Christian higher education. Lecturers have come from diverse Christian traditions, including Baptist, Christian Reformed, Church of Christ, Lutheran, Methodist, Presbyterian, and Quaker. Sharing commitment to Christ and to the project of Christian higher education, they have informed, provoked, and inspired thousands through their contributions to the Hester Lecture Series. For H. I. Hester's leadership and generosity, we remain indebted.

We also express appreciation to Martin Gallagher, Kristen Hanson, Travis Pardo, and Wynne Vinueza for timely, conscientious research assistance — work often involving some tedium, but always completed cheerfully.

To countless colleagues, friends, teachers, and family members who

ACKNOWLEDGMENTS

formed us in Christian faith and life, we owe more than can be said. Paul commands, "Anyone who receives instruction in the word must share all good things with his instructor" (Gal. 6:6). In the small endeavor this book represents, we hope to begin fulfilling this charge, for our instructors near and far.

ᴤ

Introduction

BOB R. AGEE AND DOUGLAS V. HENRY

With growing earnestness and understanding, Christian scholars of late
have explored better ways of relating Christian faith to various academic
disciplines. Many have with new energy conducted research and published work concerning the implications of Christian faith for their disciplines, and have done so at the level of presuppositions, methodologies, and conclusions. Others have attended to what it takes for
institutions with roots in a faith heritage to be unapologetically Christian
in their approach to the teaching and learning process. George Marsden,
Mark Noll, Richard Hughes, Joel Carpenter, Robert Benne, Arthur
Holmes, Robert Sloan, and countless others have emerged as leaders in
the effort to stimulate thought about the important task of expressing
Christian faith in the academic world. As books and papers and lecturers
on the issues have become more visible, a host of major issues have been
raised.

Not least among these issues is a sharpened awareness of the need
for Christian voices in various academic disciplines, for such voices have
the potential to advance learning and enrich Christian understanding
while witnessing to the love of God with heart, soul, and mind. The opportunities for Christian engagement with important academic issues
are legion. For example, the failure to distinguish between metaphysical
and methodological naturalism has often fostered unnecessary points of
tension between science and religion. That scientists embrace the latter
by no means entails that they countenance the former, a point with nu-

merous implications for the study of biological evolution, cosmology, and the environment. In the social sciences, a well-formed Christian anthropology can help critique reductive accounts of human behavior and methods for dealing with human behavior, such as those that undermine moral responsibility by presuming a deterministic behaviorism. In the professional disciplines, matters of practice can and often do generate tension between state of the art technique and the teachings of Scripture, and call for perceptive theological analysis in the service of Christian faithfulness. In short, the Christian faith bears significance for the way we understand our world, the way we address human development, the way we define humanity's place on the planet, and the way we explain the pilgrimage and destiny of humanity.

Perhaps unfortunately, there is no clear-cut, universally agreed upon way of being responsive as Christian academics to our different disciplines. There is no creed that tells us how points of tension should be understood or resolved. The nuances of Scripture, the profundity of the faith, and the complexity of the world render formulaic prescriptions for integrating faith and learning trite at best, and misleading at worst. This means that the very thing for which needs are greatest is also among the more difficult endeavors of Christian intellectual faithfulness.

To make matters worse, few faculty have had the opportunity during their graduate studies to think through these issues in any kind of formal way. Most faculty with terminal degrees pursue their graduate education in secular settings. Because mainstream graduate schools tend toward apathy — and occasionally antipathy — regarding Christian faith and thought, Christian graduate students likewise tend to avoid making their faith a central category by which to organize their academic efforts. In some fields, great emphasis is placed upon "objectivity," with the result that admitting value judgments or personal perspective into one's work is proscribed, notwithstanding the impossibility of a "view from nowhere." Consequently, not enough faculty come to the project of Christian higher education having had sufficient occasions to talk with others about the significance of Christian faith for their disciplines. The end result can be the formation of fine Christian persons competent in their fields, but who lack understanding of the ways that Christian faith should shape their work.

Further, hiring professors who have sound academic credentials and who are active members of Christian churches does not guarantee that

Christian education is going to take place. Contemporary culture makes it easier than ever to fragment life so that people can profess strong religious belief on Sunday, but see it as having little bearing on what they do in their work. Academicians are no exception to this trend toward compartmentalization, and active efforts are needed to combat it.

For all of these reasons and more, we must conscientiously, deliberately explore the relationship of Christian faith to the various disciplines within the academy, engaging one another in dialogue and debate about how to realize fidelity to biblically based Christian faith, and doing so not in spite of but precisely because of our scholarly vocation. Such dialogue should not attempt to produce a uniform set of simple solutions to the dilemmas. Reductionism is unproductive whether or not it derives from Christian sources. Such exploration can, however, help to make us more aware of the hazards of ideas that are unfaithful to the Lord; more sensitive to our students and to the biases, prejudices, and perspectives they bring to our classrooms; and more prepared to model well-integrated Christian commitment of heart, soul, and mind within and without the church.

The profession of scholar/teacher has attracted a multitude of dedicated Christian believers who will welcome the opportunity to explore faith issues within their fields of study. We believe that God calls people into the teaching and scholarly professions just as much as he does to any ministerial or missionary profession. Many have found such calling lived out by teaching within an institution with an unapologetic Christian faith heritage and perspective. Others have found their calling lived out within public colleges and universities. The issues raised in this book are not limited in significance to those who teach within the church-related college or university. They are much broader in scope and appeal to any Christian scholar/teacher willing to contemplate and converse about what it means to be Christian in the academic world.

It is our hope that this edited volume will encourage continued attention to the faith and learning emphasis so important to the revitalization of the Christian academy. It is our further hope that academic leaders will make the study of faith and learning issues an ongoing component of faculty development programs. The issues are so numerous, and the Christian faith so comprehensive in scope and application, that it will take more than our lifetimes to exhaust the topics of concern.

Faithful Learning and the Christian Scholarly Vocation helps in this effort by exploring the relationship between Christian faith and intellectual life. It offers a theological foundation for understanding the motives, aims, and practice of faith and learning integration within the academy, and then goes on to consider some of the important intellectual challenges and opportunities faced by Christian higher education in the twenty-first century. Chapters in the first section survey the nature and shape of Christian higher education, attending to the theological imperative to integrate faith and learning. Specific issues broached include the theological resources borne within varied Christian traditions for the intellectual life, the professorate as a response to God's call, and the relation of Christian higher education to the mission of the church. Contributions in the second section examine challenges and opportunities presently faced by Christian higher education, including the erosion of public trust in higher education, escalating moral relativism, the proliferation of narcissistic and self-indulgent behaviors, and the likelihood of increased conflict among civilizations. Reflection questions at the end of each chapter prompt thoughtful reading and provide stimulus for collaborative discussion of the most critical issues of Christian higher education.

Varied academic disciplines, theological perspectives, and practical experiences are united in this volume, useful for faculty, students, and patrons of Christian higher education alike. The book encourages reflective action on the part of its readers, showing that faith and learning integration must not be merely institutional rhetoric, armchair recreation, or pedagogical postscript, but the *sine qua non* of Christian higher education. For this reason, we hope that you, like Augustine of Hippo, will not only hear a word to "take up and read," but having done so, will also live out through keen awareness, careful discussion, hard work, and joyous accomplishment the highest ideals of Christian scholarly faithfulness.

Part One

Theological Reflection

Chapter One

Christian Faith and the Life of the Mind

RICHARD T. HUGHES

How is it possible for Christian colleges and universities to mature into absolutely first rate institutions of higher learning while, at the very same time, living out of the faith traditions that gave them birth? In the field of Christian higher education, no question could be more urgent, for throughout the course of Western history, numerous institutions of higher learning, originally founded to serve both the life of the mind and the Christian faith, have sloughed off their Christian underpinnings when they became academically respectable. I am convinced that this pattern does not imply that Christian faith and the life of the mind are fundamentally incompatible. But it does suggest that Christian educators have often failed to ask in meaningful ways, What is there in the Christian faith that can sustain serious intellectual inquiry and the life of the mind?

So let me frame the question with which we will be dealing in terms that I hope will be unmistakably clear. I am not asking, How is it possible

---

This chapter was presented as the H. I. Hester Lecture Series for the June 14-16, 1998, meeting of the ASBCS. Versions of this material have appeared in *Intersections* (Winter 1998), a publication serving the academic communities of the colleges and universities of the Evangelical Lutheran Church in America; in William M. Shea and Alice Gallin, eds., *Trying Times: American Catholic Higher Education in the Twentieth Century* (Atlanta: Scholars Press, 1998); in *The Southern Baptist Educator* (Fall 1998 and First Quarter 1999); and in *How Christian Faith Can Sustain the Life of the Mind* (Grand Rapids: Eerdmans, 2001).

for Christian faith and the life of the mind to merely coexist? If we frame the question in those terms, we are beaten before we begin, for if we ask about mere coexistence, we confess — quite wrongly, I believe — that Christian faith and serious intellectual inquiry are not really compatible partners. If we frame the question in terms of coexistence, therefore, we have set ourselves up for failure and can surely anticipate that when our institutions achieve the levels of academic excellence toward which we aspire, the faith dimensions of our colleges and universities will inevitably wither away.

I am therefore not asking about coexistence. Instead, I am asking, How can we genuinely live out of our faith commitments? Put another way, is it possible to use the faith commitments of our colleges and universities as the foundation for academic growth and maturity? Or put yet another way, is it possible to embrace serious intellectual inquiry precisely because of our Christian commitments, not in spite of those commitments?

I am convinced that the Christian faith can indeed sustain the kind of work in which each of us is engaged. But for that to happen, each of us must begin to ask in a careful and systematic way, What is there about the Christian faith, what is there about my own denominational tradition that can genuinely sustain the life of the mind? This is the question I want to explore, and I will do so with reference to five Christian traditions: Reformed, Anabaptist/Mennonite, Catholic, Lutheran, and Baptist. In each case, I want to ask what resources the tradition might bring to the task of higher education.

Before we begin, we first must ask what we mean when we use the phrase, "the life of the mind." Surely, the life of the mind has little to do with rote memorization or the manipulation of data. Instead, it has everything to do with three dimensions of human thought. First, the life of the mind commits us to a rigorous and disciplined search for truth. Second, in the context of that search, the life of the mind entails genuine conversation as we seriously engage a variety of perspectives and worldviews in our radically pluralistic world. And third, the life of the mind involves critical thinking as we seek to discriminate between those worldviews and perspectives. When we ask, therefore, how various manifestations of the Christian faith can sustain the life of the mind, we are really asking how the Christian faith can sustain the twin tasks of conversation and critical analysis in the context of the search for truth.

4

A Reformed Church Model

In what ways can the Reformed tradition sustain the life of the mind? The answer to that question has everything to do with the original vision of John Calvin. Simply put, Calvin sought to transform Geneva, Switzerland, into a model kingdom of God. To achieve this goal, he sought to place every facet of Genevan life — its religion, its politics, its music, and its art — squarely under the sovereignty of God. Ever since those early days, this same vision has motivated Calvinists to bring all human life and culture under the sovereign sway of God's control. Abraham Kuyper, the Dutch statesman and philosopher, expressed this vision well: "There is not a square inch on the whole plain of human existence over which Christ, who is Lord over all, does not proclaim: 'This is Mine!'"[1]

Clearly, the passion to transform human culture into the kingdom of God is the driving genius of the Reformed tradition, and it is precisely this vision that sustains the life of the mind in many Reformed institutions of higher learning. Reformed educators seek to place the entire curriculum — and every course within the curriculum — under the sovereignty of God. According to this vision, all learning should be Christian in both purpose and orientation. For this reason, Reformed educators employ three fundamental concepts that underscore these objectives.

The first and most important of those concepts is a notion popularized by Abraham Kuyper, the notion of a Christian worldview. As Albert Wolters points out, Kuyper argued that "Calvinism was not just a theology or a system of ecclesiastical polity but a complete worldview with implications for all of life, implications which must be worked out and applied in such areas as politics, art, and scholarship." With such a worldview, Kuyper believed, Christianity could provide broad cultural leadership in the nineteenth century and compete head to head with other perspectives like socialism or Darwinism or positivism.[2]

---

1. Abraham Kuyper, "Souvereiniteit in Eigen Kring" (Amsterdam: Kruyt, 1880), p. 32, cited in James D. Bratt and Ronald A. Wells, "Piety and Progress: A History of Calvin College," in *Models for Christian Higher Education: Strategies for Survival and Success in the Twenty-First Century,* ed. Richard T. Hughes and William B. Adrian (Grand Rapids: Eerdmans, 1997), p. 143.

2. Albert Wolters, "On the Idea of Worldview and Its Relation to Philosophy," in *Stained Glass: Worldviews and Social Science,* ed. Paul A. Marshall, Sander Griffioen, and Richard J. Mouw (New York: University Press of America, 1989), p. 20.

Central to the notion of a Christian worldview stands the second conviction, the notion that all truth is God's truth. By this phrase, Reformed educators mean to say that God is the author not only of our faith, but also of every facet of the world in which we live. If this is true, then there can be no discrepancy between Christian convictions and authentic knowledge regarding other aspects of human life. It is therefore possible to understand every facet of the natural sciences, the social sciences, and religion and the humanities in the light of Christian faith without running the risk of intellectual dishonesty. It is precisely this conviction that breathes life into the third concept employed by Reformed educators: the integration of faith and learning. Because all truth is God's truth, all learning should be integrated into a coherent understanding of reality, informed by explicitly Christian convictions. Arthur Holmes has expressed the theological rationale for this perspective superbly in his classic book, *The Idea of a Christian College*. There, he argues:

> When the apostle writes that in Christ "are hid all the treasures of wisdom and knowledge" (Col. 2:3), he refers . . . to [the fact that] Jesus Christ is . . . Creator and Lord of every created thing. All our knowledge of anything comes into focus around that fact. We see nature, persons, society, and the arts and sciences in proper relationship to their divine Creator and Lord. . . . The truth is a coherent whole by virtue of the common focus that ties it all into one.[3]

It is incumbent, therefore, upon Reformed educators to integrate explicitly Christian convictions into every branch of learning and, more than that, to discover those common, Christocentric threads that transform all fields of learning into one coherent whole.

Finally, this triad of ideas — a Christian worldview, all truth is God's truth, and the integration of faith and learning — sustains another notion that is critical to at least one version of the Reformed understanding of reality: the notion of secularization. The truth is, one finds in the Reformed tradition two perspectives on this theme. First, Calvin himself argued that "the Spirit of God [is] the sole fountain of truth," whether one finds that truth in the secular sphere or in divine

3. Arthur Holmes, *The Idea of a Christian College,* rev. ed. (Grand Rapids: Eerdmans, 1987), p. 17.

revelation.[4] At the same time, following another impulse in Calvin, many contemporary Reformed thinkers view the secular as a hindrance to the Christian presence in the world and therefore seek to overcome it by transforming it into the kingdom of God.[5]

From this latter perspective, secularization occurs when we see even one dimension of human life outside the sovereignty of God, or when we fail to bring all of reality under the umbrella of a distinctly Christian worldview. Because the possibility of secularization is so real in this context, the notion of a slippery slope is a metaphor that many in this tradition take very seriously. This means that if one hopes to avoid the slippery slope toward secularization, the integration of faith and learning around a distinctly Christian worldview becomes absolutely imperative.

This aspect of the Reformed tradition stands in stark relief when we compare it with Lutheranism, on the one hand, and Catholicism, on the other. For if some in the Reformed tradition argue that the slippery slope to secularization is a real and present danger, both the Lutheran and Catholic traditions acknowledge the secular as a legitimate vehicle of the grace of God.

Now we must finally ask, How can the Reformed tradition sustain the life of the mind? Clearly, it does so by integrating faith and learning around a distinctly Christian worldview. One can identify at least two great strengths of this perspective, whether one subscribes to the Reformed worldview or not. In the first place, it overcomes fragmentation with its holistic approach to learning. And in the second place, it provides students with a clearly defined standpoint from which they can discriminate between competing perspectives and worldviews. And if one cares about relating faith to learning at all, one is likely to find the Reformed emphasis on the sovereignty of God over the entire learning process extraordinarily compelling.

But to what extent does the Reformed perspective encourage academic freedom and genuine interaction with pluralism and diversity? There are two answers to that question. First, if a given scholar embraces

4. John Calvin, *Institutes of the Christian Religion,* 2.2.15, ed. John T. McNeill and trans. Ford Lewis Battles, *The Library of Christian Classics,* vol. 20 (Philadelphia: Westminster, 1960), pp. 273-75.

5. See Nicholas Wolterstorff's important discussion of the role of the secular in Reformed thought in *Until Justice and Peace Embrace* (Grand Rapids: Eerdmans, 1983), p. 12 and pp. 40-41.

the Reformed worldview, and is willing to understand all reality from the standpoint of that perspective, he or she will experience substantial academic freedom. Arthur Holmes, among others, has made this point abundantly clear:

> Academic freedom is valuable only when there is a prior commitment to the truth. And commitment to the truth is fully worthwhile only when that truth exists in One who transcends both the relativity of human perspectives and the fears of human concern.[6]

On the other hand, while the Reformed perspective allows the scholar substantial freedom to search for penultimate truths within the context of an all-embracing Christian worldview, the Reformed perspective is always susceptible to the twin risks of triumphalism and distortion. A hypothetical case in point might be a class in world religions. How, for example, would one study Buddhism from the standpoint of a Christian worldview without either distorting Buddhism into something it is not or debunking Buddhism in favor of a triumphalist Christian perspective?

And yet, the Reformed tradition contains at its core a powerful conviction that can undermine triumphalism. That conviction is simply the historic Reformed insistence on the finitude and brokenness of humankind and of all human thinking and constructions. Arthur Holmes points squarely to that principle when he writes, "Truth is not yet fully known; every academic discipline is subject to change, correction, and expansion — even theology."[7] Holmes further notes that even worldview construction must take on tentative dimensions. A Christian worldview, he argues, is merely "exploratory, not a closed system worked out once and for all but an endless undertaking. . . . It remains open-ended because the task is so vast that to complete it would require the omniscience of God."[8] At the same time, the Reformed notion that God has called upon his saints to renovate the world is such an overpowering theme that the profoundly Calvinist theme of human finitude and brokenness can sometimes get lost in the shuffle.

6. Holmes, *The Idea of a Christian College,* p. 69.
7. Holmes, *The Idea of a Christian College,* p. 66.
8. Holmes, *The Idea of a Christian College,* pp. 58-59, 66.

An Anabaptist/Mennonite Model

When we turn from the Reformed to the Anabaptist/Mennonite tradition, we quickly discover that we have entered into a frame of reference radically different from the Reformed perspective. The first thing we notice is that the starting point for Mennonites has more to do with holistic living than cognition, more to do with ethics than intellect. One faculty member at Goshen College summarized very nicely the difference between the Reformed and Mennonite models when she observed that if the Reformed model is fundamentally cerebral and transforms living by thinking, the Mennonite model transforms thinking by living.

More precisely, Mennonites begin their task by seeking to implement a vision of discipleship that takes its cue from the radical teachings of Jesus. They take seriously Jesus' words when he counseled his followers to abandon self in the interest of others, or when he charged his disciples to practice humility, simplicity, and nonviolence. Theirs is a radical vision, to be sure, and one that stands almost entirely out of sync with the values of the larger culture.

One who is not accustomed to the Mennonite frame of reference might well ask what this perspective has to do with the life of the mind. How can unconventional virtues like these possibly sustain the values we associate with the academy? Put another way, how does one move from Christocentric living to critical and pluralistic thinking?

We can answer that question in three ways. First, we must recall that sixteenth-century Anabaptism originated in the very womb of dissent. In a world that prized lockstep uniformity, Anabaptists dared to question the status quo. It matters little that their dissent began with lifestyle commitments rather than high-level theoretical formulations. Regardless of their starting point, sixteenth-century Anabaptists proved time and again their commitment to independent thinking. If a willingness to question conventional wisdom stands at the heart of the academic enterprise, then surely the Anabaptist heritage offers important resources for sustaining the life of the mind.

Second, Mennonites routinely counsel one another to abandon self in the interest of others and to abandon narrow nationalism in the interest of world citizenship. For this reason, service to other human beings, especially to the poor, the marginalized, and the oppressed throughout the world, stands at the heart of the Mennonite witness. If we ask how a global service commitment like this can sustain the life of the mind, the answer is not hard to find. It is difficult to abandon self for the sake of others in any meaningful sense unless one is prepared to take seriously those "others," their cultural contexts, and their points of view. This means that Mennonite colleges, precisely because of their service orientation, are prepared to take seriously one of the cardinal virtues of the modern academy: the emphasis on pluralism and diversity.

If one wishes to see how this commitment might play itself out in an academic context, one need only consider the international studies program at Goshen College where eighty percent of all students spend one entire semester in a Third World culture where they serve, on the one hand, and seek to learn that country's history, cultural traditions, and language, on the other.

Finally, because of its historic emphasis on humility, the Mennonite tradition prepares its scholars to embrace one of the cardinal virtues of the academic guild: the willingness to admit that my understandings may be fragmentary and incomplete and that, indeed, I could be wrong.

For all these reasons, the Mennonite commitment to a life of radical discipleship can contribute in substantial ways to a vigorous life of the mind. Yet, we must also acknowledge that while the Mennonite commitment to stand with a radical Jesus is surely one of their greatest strengths, it can also be a serious liability in the arena of higher education. Ironically, the very commitment that has often inspired humility, dissent, and respect for cultural diversity can also inspire narrowness and sectarian exclusivity. This can happen in several ways, when Mennonites, for example, allow the radical teachings of Jesus to become little more than the substance of ethnic folkways, or when Mennonites take seriously the ethical mandates of Jesus without embracing with equal seriousness the grace of God whereby he forgives us in spite of our failings and shortcomings.

A Roman Catholic Model

When we ask about a Roman Catholic model for higher education the first thing we notice is the diversity that characterizes Catholic institutions of higher learning. After all, Catholic colleges and universities were established not by the church *per se* but by a variety of religious orders that bring to the task of higher education a diversity of emphases. Nonetheless, we find in all Catholic colleges and universities certain uniquely Catholic dimensions that sustain the life of the mind.

The first of these dimensions is the sacramental principle that points to the fact that the natural world and even elements of human culture can serve as vehicles by which the grace of God is mediated to human beings. This conviction allows Catholic educators to take the world seriously on its own terms and to interact with the world as it is.

If some Reformed educators argue that the world and the contents of human culture are fundamentally secular if not brought under the sovereign sway of the Lord Jesus Christ, many Catholic educators, affirming the sacramental principle, take sharp issue with that contention. Alice Gallin, former executive director of the Association for Catholic Colleges and Universities, for example, has argued that "'secular' is not simply nor always the opposite of 'sacred,' for in a Christian sacramental view of reality, the secular has a legitimate role and one that is congruent with and not opposed to faith or religion."[9] This is why David O'Brien of the College of the Holy Cross points to one of the documents of Vatican II, *The Pastoral Constitution on the Church and the Modern World,* as a virtual "magna charta" for Catholic colleges and universities. It functions in this way, O'Brien argued, since it affirms "the study of the human sciences, respect for non-Catholic, secular culture, dialogue with those beyond the church, and service to society," all in the context of the sacramental principle.[10]

In a word, the sacramental principle sustains the life of the mind by placing a very great value both on the natural world and on human culture, and by reminding us that these realms are fully legitimate, whether transformed by the rule of Christ or not. For this reason, the notion of a slippery slope to secularization scarcely makes sense in a Roman Catholic context.

The second characteristic that allows the Catholic tradition to sustain the life of the mind is the universality of the Catholic faith. As a

9. Alice Gallin, "American Church Related Higher Education: Comparison and Contrast," ACHE presentation, December 29, 1992, p. 1.

10. David O'Brien, *From the Heart of the American Church: Catholic Higher Education and American Culture* (Maryknoll, N.Y.: Orbis, 1994), p. 49.

global church, Catholicism embraces believers from every corner of the world, people who hold a variety of political ideologies, who speak a myriad of tongues, who represent virtually every nationality in the world, and who reflect every social and economic class on the planet today. Not only is Catholicism universal in this very tangible sense; it is also intentionally universal from a theological point of view.

The universality of the Catholic tradition should permit the Catholic university to prize pluralism and diversity and to find a legitimate place at the table for every conversation partner. Many have argued this case, but no one has done so more effectively than Fr. Theodore Hesburgh, President Emeritus of the University of Notre Dame. "The Catholic university," Hesburgh writes, "must be a bridge across all the chasms that separate modern people from each other: the gaps between young and old, men and women, rich and poor, black and white, believer and unbeliever, potent and weak, east and west, material and spiritual, scientist and humanist, developed and less developed, and all the rest. To be such a mediator, the Catholic university, as universal, must be engaged with, and have an interest in, both edges of every gulf, must understand each, encompass each in its total community and build a bridge of understanding and love."[11]

This notion of the Catholic university as bridge, rooted in the universality of the Catholic faith, can play itself out in some very concrete ways, most notably in faculty hiring policies. On the one hand, Notre Dame has sought to create that bridge by hiring not only a diversity of faculty from a variety of faith traditions and no tradition at all, but also by insuring "the continuing presence of a predominant number of Catholic intellectuals" on the faculty, as the university's president mandated in 1993.[12] On the other hand, many Catholic institutions, grounding themselves in that same concern for universality, demonstrate little or no concern with this issue. David O'Brien reports, for example, that "a Jesuit dean [at Georgetown] told the faculty that, while wisdom rooted in faith remained central at Georgetown, 'a person's religion plays no part in hiring, tenure, promotion, the awarding of grants

11. Theodore M. Hesburgh, "The Challenge and Promise of a Catholic University," in *The Challenge and Promise of a Catholic University,* ed. T. M. Hesburgh (Notre Dame: University of Notre Dame Press, 1994), pp. 9-10.

12. O'Brien, *From the Heart of the American Church,* p. 91.

or the securing of funds. In fact, most of us don't know each other's religious beliefs.'"[13]

The final Catholic commitment I wish to consider is one Monika Hellwig describes as the communitarian nature of redemption. At its core, this notion holds that the church is not simply the hierarchical magisterium; instead, the church is comprised of all the people of God, scattered throughout the world, who together form this community of faith. This means that the life of the mind, if understood only in cognitive terms, is less than adequate in a Catholic university. Instead, as Hellwig notes, the life of the mind must translate itself into genuine "bonds of friendship and mutual respect and support [which] are envisaged as the core of the educational enterprise, because not only book learning but human formation for leadership and responsibility in all walks of life are sought through the community experience of higher education."[14]

Precisely because it takes "seriously the unity of the human race," the communitarian dimension suggests that Catholic colleges and universities should place scholarship and teaching in the service of justice and peace for all the peoples of the world. To a great extent, Catholic institutions — and especially Jesuit institutions — have done just that. As David O'Brien observes, "president after president [in the world of Catholic higher education] has repeated the words of the American bishops insisting that pursuit of justice and human dignity is an essential work of a Catholic institution."[15]

It is clear that the Roman Catholic tradition is at home with human reason, with the natural world, with secular human culture, with human history, with human beings who stand both inside and outside of the Catholic faith, and with human beings in every conceivable social circumstance. It is precisely this dimension that renders the Catholic faith, at least in theory, so compatible with the ideals of the modern university.

At the same time, it is entirely possible for the Catholic tradition to stand at odds with the life of the mind. This can happen when dogma

13. O'Brien, *From the Heart of the American Church,* p. 90. Also see Emmanuel Renner and Hilary Thimmesh, "Faith and Learning at the College of Saint Benedict and Saint John's University," in *Models for Christian Higher Education,* pp. 42-43.

14. Monika K. Hellwig, "What Can the Roman Catholic Tradition Contribute to Christian Higher Education?" in *Models for Christian Higher Education,* p. 21.

15. O'Brien, *From the Heart of the American Church,* pp. 86-87.

displaces inquiry, when orthodoxy undermines the search for truth, or when Catholics absolutize those dimensions of Catholic faith that might otherwise have the potential to break through their own particularity.

A Lutheran Model

The Lutheran tradition offers its own strong resources for sustaining the life of the mind. The first resource is Luther's insistence on human finitude and the sovereignty of God. To speak of human finitude is to point not only to our frailties, our limitations, and our estrangement from God, from other human beings, and even from ourselves; it also points to the depth and breadth of sin that renders us incapable of knowing or doing the good. When Luther argues for God's sovereignty, therefore, his point is not that Christians should impose God's sovereignty on an unbelieving world. That would be an impossible absurdity. Rather, when Luther points to God's sovereignty, he always points at the very same time to human finitude. The sovereignty of God, therefore, means that I am not God, that my reason is inevitably impaired, and that my knowledge is always fragmentary and incomplete.

In the context of higher education and the life of the mind, this position means that every scholar must always confess that he or she could be wrong. Apart from this confession, there can be no serious life of the mind, for only when we confess that we might be wrong can we engage in the kind of conversation that takes seriously other voices. Further, it is only when we confess that we might be wrong that we are empowered to scrutinize critically our own theories, judgments, and understandings. Put another way, in the Lutheran tradition, doubt is always the partner of faith. In his marvelous book, *Exiles from Eden,* Mark Schwehn quotes James Gustafson to the effect that "we believe what we question and question what we believe."[16] Or, as the father of the boy with the evil spirit confessed to Jesus in Mark 9, "Lord, I believe; help thou mine unbelief." One who refuses to confess that he or she might be wrong has forfeited the ability to engage in critical scholarship and really has no legitimate place in the academy.

16. Mark Schwehn, *Exiles from Eden: Religion and the Academic Vocation in America* (New York: Oxford University Press, 1993), p. 49.

Because of the Lutheran insistence on human finitude, Lutheran theology always has the capacity to break through its own particularity. Authentic Lutherans can never absolutize their own perspectives, even their theological perspectives. They must always be reassessing and re-thinking, and they must always be in dialogue with themselves and with others. This is the genius of the Lutheran tradition, and this is the first reason why the Lutheran tradition can sustain the life of the mind.

The second resource the Lutheran tradition offers for sustaining the life of the mind is Luther's notion of paradox, a theme that stands at the heart of Lutheran thought. Luther gloried in the notion of paradox: the King of the universe born in a manger, God himself nailed to a Roman cross, the Christian who is both free and servant at one and the same time, and the Christian who is simultaneously justified and a sinner. But of all of Luther's paradoxes, there is none more supportive of the life of the mind than his notion of the two kingdoms. In his view, the Christian lives in the world and in the kingdom of God — or, put another way, in nature and in grace — and does so simultaneously. In fact, in Luther's vision, God employs the finite dimensions of the natural world as vehicles that convey his grace to human beings. As Luther often affirmed, *finitum capax infiniti* — the finite is the bearer of the infinite. At this point, the Lutheran tradition greatly resembles Catholic sacramental under-standings.

The authentic Lutheran vision, therefore, never calls for Lutherans to transform the secular world into the kingdom of God as many in the Reformed tradition have advocated over the years. Nor does it call for Lutherans to separate from the world as the heirs of the Anabaptists sometimes seek to do. Instead, the Christian must reside in two worlds at one and the same time: the world of nature and the world of grace. The Christian in Luther's view, therefore, is free to take seriously both the secular world and the kingdom of God.

This notion carries great implications for the life of the mind, espe-cially if we think of the life of the mind as one that fosters genuine con-versation in which all the voices at the table are taken seriously. Clearly, in the Lutheran context, there is a "Christian worldview." But in the light of Luther's two kingdoms, there is no need to impose that worldview on other voices. Nor is it important to "integrate faith and learning" around that perspective. Rather, one seeks to bring the secular world and a Christian perspective into conversation with one another.

Luther's notion of the two kingdoms is therefore fully capable of sustaining a commitment to the Christian faith and a serious engagement with the secular world at one and the same time. For this reason, the notion of a slippery slope to secularization makes no sense in a Lutheran context.

While the Lutheran tradition possesses extraordinary resources for sustaining the life of the mind, the strength of the Lutheran tradition is also its weakness. As we have seen, the notion of paradox is central to the Lutheran tradition, but it is all too easy to sacrifice one side of the paradox in the interest of the other. When the paradox dissolves in this way, the risks can be absolutism on the one hand and relativism on the other. These temptations are especially apparent when one considers Luther's understanding of the two kingdoms. If we accentuate the kingdom of God at the expense of the secular world, we run the risk of absolutizing our religious vision. Here one thinks, for example, of the scholastic theologians who absolutized the dynamic, paradoxical qualities of Luther's thought into a rigid, airtight system. This version of Lutheran theology is simply inimical to the life of the mind. Yet, rigid codification of Lutheran thought occurs even within some Lutheran colleges. On the other hand, if we accentuate the secular world at the expense of the kingdom of God, we run the risk of relativism since we have diminished our transcendent point of reference. This means that if Lutheran colleges hope to draw on their Lutheran heritage to sustain the life of the mind, they must find some way to keep alive the heart and soul of Luther's original vision, namely, the paradox of the gospel and the affirmation of the sovereignty of God and the finitude of humankind.

A Baptist Model

To be clear once again, when we ask how the Baptist tradition can sustain the life of the mind, we are really asking how the Baptist tradition can sustain critical analysis, on the one hand, and conversation with a variety of conversation partners, on the other, all in the context of a radical commitment to search for truth. And so our question is this: Does the Baptist tradition provide us with resources that can sustain us in that task?

The Difficulty of Framing a Baptist Identity

We must acknowledge from the outset that, from one perspective at least, it will be difficult to frame satisfactory answers to this question from out of the Baptist tradition. This is not because Baptist theology provides no meaningful answers, because it does. Rather, it is because the virtue above all other virtues that stands at the heart and soul of the Baptist tradition is the historic commitment that E. Y. Mullins described as "soul competency." Mullins is the man whom Harold Bloom nominated as "the Calvin or Luther or Wesley of the Southern Baptists."[17] He claimed that "the doctrine of the soul's competency in religion under God is *the* distinctive historical significance of the Baptists." He then elaborated on that theme in several ways. "The biblical significance of the Baptists," Mullins wrote,

> is the right of private interpretation and obedience to the scriptures. The significance of the Baptists in relation to the individual is individual freedom. The ecclesiastical significance of the Baptists is a regenerated church-membership and the equality and priesthood of believers. The political significance of the Baptists is the separation of Church and State.[18]

All this Mullins summed up in his phrase, "the competency of the soul in religion under God." Another Southern Baptist summed up the notion of "soul competency" like this:

> I only know to think of soul competency in practical terms. To me it means that the individual Christian is unassailable in her interpretation of Scripture and in her own understanding of God's will for her life. It means that when someone says, "This is what the Bible means to me," I cannot tell her she is wrong.[19]

While not every Baptist would understand the doctrine of soul competency in such radical terms, it is clear that at least some do. The difficulty this notion poses for the task we are undertaking must be obvious. If ev-

17. Harold Bloom, *The American Religion: The Emergence of the Post-Christian Nation* (New York: Simon and Schuster, 1992), p. 199.

18. E. Y. Mullins, *Baptist Beliefs* (Valley Forge, Pa.: Judson Press, 1912), p. 57.

19. Cited in Bloom, *The American Religion,* p. 202.

ery Baptist is finally free to read and interpret the Scriptures for himself or herself, then who can say what it really means to be a Baptist? Glenn Hinson commented perceptively on this point in one of his essays in the book, *Are Southern Baptists "Evangelicals"?* There Hinson notes that "Baptists have about as much difficulty defining who . . . [they] are as do the Evangelicals." As a result, there are just "about as many definitions [of what it means to be Baptist] as there are Baptists."[20]

If, therefore, we ask how the Baptist theological heritage can sustain the life of the mind, we encounter problems from the outset. What do we mean by "Baptist theological heritage"? Obviously, the notion of *sola scriptura* stands at the heart of the Baptist heritage. But that affirmation hardly defines what it means to be a Baptist, since the principle of soul competency allows each and every Baptist at least in theory to understand the biblical text as he or she sees fit.

This problem stands in stark relief when we compare Baptist institutions of higher learning with colleges and universities related to confessional traditions like the Missouri Synod Lutherans or the Christian Reformed Church. Go to Calvin College, for example, and ask a group of faculty — as I once did — "What does it mean when Calvin College proclaims itself a Christian institution of higher learning?" You will hear a clear, succinct, and carefully thought-out response, reflecting a virtual unanimity of sentiment. But go to a typical Baptist college or university and raise with a group of faculty that very same question, and you will hear a bewildering array of answers, reflecting the one commitment those Baptist faculty share in common as their allegiance to the principle of "soul competency" or "freedom in Christ."

Exploring the Theme of Freedom

If this is true, then perhaps we should simply ask, In what way can the venerable Baptist theme of soul competency or Christian freedom sustain the life of the mind? Based on what we know of early Baptist history, it would appear that this theme can sustain the life of the mind in powerful ways. Recall, for example, Thomas Helwys, who submitted to

20. E. Glenn Hinson, "Baptists and Evangelicals: What Is the Difference?" in *Are Southern Baptists "Evangelicals"?* ed. James Leo Garrett, Jr., E. Glenn Hinson, and James E. Tull (Macon, Ga.: Mercer University Press, 1983), p. 173.

King James I what amounted to an absolutely astounding defense of religious freedom and toleration as early as 1612:

> Our lord the king is but an earthly king, and he hath no authority as a king but in earthly causes, and if the king's people be obedient and true subjects, obeying all humane laws made by the king, our lord the king can require no more: for men's religion to God, is betwixt God and themselves; the king shall not answer for it, neither may the king be judge between God and man. Let them be heretikes, Turcks, Jewes or whatsoever, it apperteynes not to the earthly power to punish them in the least measure.[21]

Or remember the classic defense of religious freedom that Roger Williams offered to the world in his *Bloudy Tenent of Persecution:*

> It is the will and command of God that, since the coming of his Son the Lord Jesus, a permission of the most Paganish, Jewish, Turkish, or antichristian consciences and worships be granted to all men in all nations and countries: and they are only to be fought against with that sword which is only, in soul matters, able to conquer: to wit, the sword of God's Spirit, the word of God.[22]

The truth is, we can hardly imagine more powerful resources for sustaining the life of the mind in our modern world than the resources we find in these seventeenth-century Baptist defenses of religious freedom. This is particularly true if we understand the modern university as an institution that takes seriously cultural, religious, and political diversity. Every perspective has a right to exist, Helwys and Williams affirm. "Let them be heretikes, Turcks, Jewes or whatsoever," Helwys argues. And Williams will extend "a permission of the most Paganish, Jewish, Turkish, or antichristian consciences and worships . . . to all men in all nations and countries." Then Williams offers a prescription for what must surely lie at the heart of every modern university worthy of the name: we contend with ideas that are different from our own, not with coercion, but with persuasion and reasoned argument. On first glance,

---

21. Thomas Helwys, *A Short Declaration of the Mistery of Iniquity* (1612; reprinted in London by Kingsgate Press, 1935), p. 69.

22. Roger Williams, *The Bloudy Tenent of Persecution,* ed. Edward Bean Underhill (London: J. Haddon, 1848), p. 2.

then, the Baptist tradition has some of the strongest resources for sustaining the life of the mind that one could possibly imagine.

Yet, I want to suggest that the Baptist notion of soul competency, or Christian freedom, as that idea is often framed by Baptist theoreticians, may be inadequate to sustain the life of the mind in a Baptist institution of higher learning. This is simply because the notion of freedom in Baptist life and heritage has come to reflect political and cultural presuppositions fully as much as it reflects theological presuppositions. Put another way, when most of us think of freedom in the Baptist context, theological understandings seldom come to mind. Instead, we think of dissenters like Helwys and Williams, or persecuted Baptists who braved the odds to claim religious freedom in colonial Virginia and Massachusetts. This means that soul competency often gets connected in our modern imagination with claims of religious liberty for the individual or with civic virtues like separation of church and state, but seldom prompts consideration of distinctly theological notions like justification by grace through faith. In the modern Baptist imagination, the civic ends often displace theological means.

We can only admire the historic Baptist struggle on behalf of separation of church and state and freedom for religious faith and practice. But we must also admit that this historic Baptist emphasis, as strange as it may seem, may finally provide resources for the life of the mind that are quite fragile. It is plain to see why this is true. Assertions of human freedom are just that: assertions of human freedom. And unless those assertions are grounded at every step of the way in transcendent theological presuppositions, they lack the power to nurture a sustained commitment to the academic enterprise and the life of the mind. In truth, cut loose from their theological presuppositions, assertions of human freedom can all too easily be placed in the service of the broader culture, on the one hand, or limited self-interest, on the other.

Soul Competency and the Baptist Theological Heritage

I want to suggest, therefore, that if Baptist colleges and universities hope to find, in their own rich tradition, resources that can sustain the life of the mind, they must allow the traditional Baptist notion of soul competency to function, not so much as a shibboleth, or even as a traditional Baptist formulation, but rather as a window that can open widely on the rich theological resources to which all Baptists are heir.

The truth is, among those Protestant traditions that descend from the period of the Reformation, Baptists are unique. For Baptists are not a singular, one-dimensional tradition, but instead draw nourishment from all three of the major Reformation traditions considered above. In part, this is because Baptists came late to the Reformation. Baptists, alone, therefore, were able to incorporate into their identity some of the principles that were so basic to the Reformed tradition, to the Lutherans, and to the Anabaptists. For this reason, Baptist institutions of higher learning can draw on the very same resources that sustain the life of the mind in Reformed institutions, in Lutheran institutions, and in Mennonite institutions.

But the central piece of the puzzle that we must not forget is this: the Baptist doctrine of soul competency is the very window that opens wide onto each of these traditions. In the first place, the soul is competent before God and every believer is free from human coercion because God alone is sovereign. He is our God and we are his people, and we therefore owe our allegiance to him alone. This is the great contribution the Reformed tradition makes to the Baptist heritage.

Second, the soul is competent before God and every believer is free because we are not constrained by works of the law. Rather, we are justified by grace through faith. We are therefore free to take intellectual risks, to explore the outer limits of human knowledge, and even to confess that we may be wrong. This is the great contribution the Lutheran tradition makes to the Baptist heritage.

And third, the soul is competent before God and every believer is free because we believe we must obey God rather than men. Like the Anabaptists of the sixteenth century, we are therefore willing to defy all human authorities who would compel us to worship the creature rather than the Creator. This is the great contribution the Anabaptist tradition makes to the Baptist heritage. And so we see that the Baptist doctrine of soul competency is much, much more than a Baptist shibboleth or a stale, domesticated tradition that has lost its power to sustain the life of the mind. Instead, it is a doctrine of enormous power, a window onto some of the richest resources of the Protestant Reformation, and for all these reasons, perhaps the most potent intellectual resource that is available to any group of church-related institutions.

For this reason, I would hope that when I next visit a Baptist college or university and sit with faculty and ask them, "What do you mean when you say this is a Baptist institution?," those faculty would respond, "It means that here, at this place, we are free to search and inquire and explore and raise the most difficult and even the most threatening kinds of questions because God alone is sovereign, because we are justified by grace through faith, and because we are convinced we must obey God rather than men." And I would hope they then would say, "We believe these things because we are Baptists who hold most dearly the principle that every soul is competent to read the Scripture and discern the truth for himself or herself, and live out that truth as he or she sees fit. This is what it means to be a Baptist institution."

Soul Competency and the Bible

But the doctrine of soul competency can serve not only as a window that opens wide onto the theological heritage of the Protestant Reformation. It is also a window that opens wide onto the Bible itself. For after all, each of the great themes of the Protestant Reformation is rooted in the biblical text.

Admittedly, Baptists have had difficulty reconciling the two great principles on which their entire tradition hangs: the primacy of an objective biblical text and the notion that every soul is competent to read and interpret the Bible for himself or for herself. But as children of the Protestant Reformation, Baptists at their best have not viewed the Bible as a static, legal text, nor have they viewed the Bible as an end in itself. Instead, Baptists at their very best have understood the Bible as a dynamic theological treatise that points beyond itself to the majesty, sovereignty, and glory of Almighty God. The historic Baptist notion of soul competency is hardly at odds with this conception of the biblical text, but instead reflects the very heart and soul of the biblical tradition. For according to this conception, the Bible is not a book whose contents we can master, but instead points us to a God who masters each of us. According to this conception, the Bible points us not to itself, but rather to the infinite God whose understanding no human being can fathom and who stands in judgment on all our claims that, somehow, we have captured ultimate truth.

This conception of the Bible leaves no place for human pride, but forces each of us to humble ourselves before the throne of God and to acknowledge with Job:

I have uttered what I did not understand
Things too wonderful for me, which I did not know. . . .
I had heard of thee by the hearing of the ear,
But now my eye sees thee;
Therefore I despise myself
And repent in dust and ashes. (Job 42:3-6)

Or again, if we allow the Bible to point beyond itself to the infinite God, we finally have no choice but to confess with Isaiah, "Woe is me! For I am lost; for I am a man of unclean lips, and I dwell in the midst of a people of unclean lips; for my eyes have seen the King, the Lord of hosts!" (Isaiah 6:5).

Can the Bible, viewed in these terms, sustain the life of the mind? Without question, it can, for if the Bible points beyond itself to the infinite God, we have no choice but to search for truth. After all, when we view ourselves in relation to God, we understand how abysmally ignorant we really are. And if the Bible points beyond itself to an infinite God, we have no choice but to engage in serious conversation with a variety of conversation partners, for we know that all perspectives may well shed light on God's eternal truth. And if the Bible points beyond itself to an infinite God, we have no choice but to engage in critical thinking, for we must now discriminate between competing worldviews and perspectives as we seek to understand more fully the nature and the glory and the will of our Creator. All of this strikes me as the very essence of that historic Baptist formulation, "the competence of the soul in religion under God."

And so now, we finally must ask once again, Does the Baptist tradition possess theological resources that can sustain the life of the mind? The answer to this question must by now be self-evident. The Baptist tradition possesses some of the richest theological resources for sustaining the life of the mind that one can possibly imagine. The venerable Baptist doctrine of soul competency is the first of those resources. But that historic vision can be an important resource only when it draws its meaning from Christian theology, not from the vagaries of cultural and political experience. Second, as children of the Protestant Reformation, Baptists can find support for the life of the mind in the Reformed understanding of the sovereignty of God, in the Lutheran understanding of justification by grace through faith, and in the Anabaptist determination to obey God rather than men. And finally, as an authentic people of the Book, Baptist scholars can find support for the life of the mind in a Bible that points beyond itself to the glories of an infinite God.

If Baptist scholars take seriously these important aspects of their heritage, they can embrace with enthusiasm all the distinctive elements of the life of the mind: a disciplined search for truth, genuine conversation with a variety of perspectives and worldviews, and critical thought and assessment. And they can do so, not in spite of their Baptist heritage, but precisely because their Baptist heritage offers them such rich resources for their intellectual tasks.

Conclusion

We have explored five Christian models for sustaining the life of the mind. We have discovered that each of these faith traditions has its own resources that can sustain the academic enterprise. At the same time, each of these traditions has weaknesses that can undermine that enterprise. If these traditions hope to build institutions of higher learning that are academically superior, and that rest on a foundation of Christian faith, the leaders of these institutions must be both discerning and intentional. They must first discern those aspects of their particular Christian heritage that will sustain the life of the mind, and those that will not. They must then work in deliberate and intentional ways as they seek to build on the great themes of their traditions that can sustain the work of the academy.

QUESTIONS FOR REFLECTION AND DISCUSSION

1. Christians through the centuries have variously thought of faith and reason as mutually exclusive, mutually compatible, or mutually beneficial. Hughes opts strongly for the latter view, rejecting both the notion that faith merely coexists with the life of the mind, as well as more extreme views holding to the incompatibility of faith and reason. Is Hughes's position right? What assets and liabilities — to both faith and reason — come with each of the possible positions?
2. Which of the five traditions outlined in this chapter most informs your own understanding of the relation between faith and learning?

24

Which — if any — is most obviously operative within your college or university? How might it more deeply and widely inform patterns of being, thinking, and acting within your institutional context?

3. For the different traditions Hughes describes, what strengths or weaknesses go unexplored? To what extent does your own tradition bear resources for ameliorating its weaknesses? Are there ways in which the strengths of other traditions could significantly enrich your own?

FURTHER RELATED WORK BY THIS AUTHOR

Hughes, Richard T., and William B. Adrian, eds. *Models for Christian Higher Education: Strategies for Success in the Twenty-First Century.* Grand Rapids: Eerdmans, 1997.

Hughes, Richard T. *How Christian Faith Can Sustain the Life of the Mind.* Grand Rapids: Eerdmans, 2001.

Chapter Two

The Calling of the Christian Scholar-Teacher

C. STEPHEN EVANS

Let me begin by saying something about the perspective that I will attempt to adopt in addressing the calling of the Christian scholar and teacher. I want to bear in mind what Christians have in common — to seek to look at things from the perspective of what C. S. Lewis called "mere Christianity." Lewis is one of my favorite authors, and *Mere Christianity* is certainly one of his best and most influential books. Whatever else may be true of Baptist, Catholic, or Methodist institutions, they must be Christian institutions, and consideration of that must be central to their identity, just as it is central to a Christian Reformed college to think of Reformed Christianity as a specific expression of the Christian faith that goes back to the apostles and ultimately to Jesus of Nazareth.

None of us would like to be in the embarrassing position detailed in a story I have heard, one that may be apocryphal but makes an important point about a former president of a prominent Methodist university. According to the story, the president gave a talk to a local Methodist organization, emphasizing the close ties between his school and the Methodist church. In the discussion period, someone asked him if he would be willing to describe his institution as a Christian university. The president said that he was not really comfortable with that description. The ques-

Evans presented the Hester Lectures at the June 5-8, 1999, ASBCS meeting; this chapter was adapted from versions in the Third Quarter 1999, Fourth Quarter 1999, and First Quarter 2000 issues of *The Southern Baptist Educator.*

tioner logically concluded: So your school is Methodist but not Christian. We do not want to put ourselves in the situation of having schools that are denominational but not Christian, and so it will be profitable to think together about what it means for an institution of higher education to be distinctively Christian. I will help do this by first reflecting upon the Christian scholar-teacher whose calling lies at the heart of the Christian college or university, and then upon the nature of the Christian scholarship to which such persons aspire.

The Crucial Importance of the Christian Scholar-Teacher

There are of course many dimensions to an authentically Christian college, university, or seminary. We could focus on the necessity for a lively spiritual life, a community united by a focus on worship and prayer, a need that in turn has multiple implications for student life, chapel, residence halls, and many other things. We could focus on the ways in which a truly Christian institution makes its faith real in its ethical relationships, both within the community and without. We could focus on the ways in which a Christian institution serves the many communities of which it is a part, including the global community. All of these and many more themes would be appropriate and important to consider. However, I have been for most of my career a member of the faculty and it is often said that the faculty lies at the heart of any educational institution. So both because it is what I know best and also because of its great importance, I want to consider the role of Christian faculty in a Christian educational institution, and to do so by exploring the noble calling of the Christian scholar-teacher.

Christian faculty members generally understand the idea that religious commitment and learning can pull us in various directions. Those of us who are Christians have experienced this from both sides. Many of us know what it is like to be under suspicion from a church community because of our scholarly learning. Many of us also know what it feels like to be under suspicion in an academic community because of our religious commitments, to have colleagues who regard us with disdain or condescension, and who question whether our commitments to religious faith compromise our scholarship. However, despite these tensions, it is possible to combine genuine religious faith with a genuine commitment to excellence in our tasks in education. If we did not think so, surely we would not have chosen to become a part of institutions that seek to maintain a Christian identity.

Nevertheless, because of these tensions, we experience pressures. Sometimes there are pressures to compromise our educational excellence or integrity in the name of what someone regards as Christian orthodoxy. Sometimes there are pressures in the other direction — subtle pressures to dilute or eliminate our distinctiveness as Christian teacher-scholars. These pressures can be resisted, for it is possible to fulfill the calling of the Christian scholar-teacher with integrity. How?

The Christian Scholar-Teacher as a Believer in Christian Higher Education

My first point may seem so obvious as not to be worth making, but I think it is so important that it cannot be passed over in silence. The Christian scholar-teacher must be a person who believes in Christian higher education, who is committed to the mission of his or her institution. It is not enough to hire faculty who happen to be Christians, even if they are fine scholars. We must find and keep faculty who are committed to the project.

Oddly enough, the people who do this best are often outsiders to the tradition that has nourished and founded the institution. People who have been brought up within a tradition are often tempted to take it for granted, or, even worse, see the religious heritage as an impediment to progress — something to react against. For example, at St. Olaf College I found that it was often the Catholics and Baptists on the faculty who worked hardest to maintain the Lutheran identity of the college, and at Calvin College I found it was often those who were converts to the Reformed faith who were most committed to its prospects and excited about its mission.

But what exactly is the Christian teacher-scholar committed to? What is the mission? Here is one way of getting at the heart of the matter, which I owe to Nicholas Wolterstorff. Without being triumphalist, Christians can and should participate in our common human cultural endeavors.[1] The uniqueness of this idea should not be taken for granted.

---

1. Wolterstorff developed this theme and many of the ideas that follow in a lecture

Without trying to play God or think that the kingdom of God can be achieved on earth through human means, we Christians must not withdraw from our common human cultural endeavors, but must strive to engage with those areas of cultural action and transform them. We must become salt and light in the midst of a world that is fallen but which God loves and wishes to redeem. Because this commitment to what we might call a transformative Christian vision is so central to the committed Christian scholar-teacher, I want to discuss one of its most powerful advocates, the Dutch theologian Abraham Kuyper (1837-1920).

Kuyper expressed a powerful vision for Christian cultural engagement. Besides being a great theologian, Kuyper founded the Free University of Amsterdam, a Christian political party, a newspaper, and Christian labor unions, all of which continue to exist. Kuyper resisted the idea that religion was something private and personal only, affirming in his speech at the dedication of the Free University that "there is not one single inch of the created world over which Jesus Christ does not say, 'This too is mine.'"[2]

Kuyper's thought is especially relevant today for a number of reasons. Kuyper lived in a country that was religiously divided. He wanted to develop a blueprint for a society which would be genuinely pluralistic, but one in which Christians are called to participate as Christians in our common human endeavors. This differs from two other common models.

There is first the model that Christians can participate in our common human endeavors (government, education, the arts, industry, etc.), but that they should not do so as Christians but simply as generic human beings. According to this model, Christians can certainly participate in our common human endeavors, but when they do so, their identity as Christians is not central to their lives. Rather, their faith is, in the words of contemporary social theorists, privatized. This model has become dominant in American society, and though it is still very appealing to many, it has many destructive consequences. It is privatized religion that allows human beings to go to church on Sundays without asking how this should affect their lives on Mondays in business, government, or

on Abraham Kuyper delivered at Calvin College. To my knowledge, this lecture is unpublished. On this theme, see also Richard J. Mouw, *He Shines in All That's Fair: Culture and Common Grace* (Grand Rapids: Eerdmans, 2001).

2. Abraham Kuyper, "Souvereiniteit in Eigen Kring" (Amsterdam: Kruyt, 1880), p. 32.

education. Kuyper wanted to find a way for Christians to participate in these human activities without shedding their primary identity and loyalty as followers of Jesus Christ.

At the other end of the continuum are those who think that Christians must always maintain their primary identity and loyalty, but that this requires them to withdraw from our common human endeavors and perhaps form separate communities. I have great respect for those such as the Amish who have chosen this path, but I believe most Christians are called to live in the world and not withdraw from it.

Kuyper rejects both of these extremes. His vision was of a pluralistic society in which Christians — in his case Reformed Christians in the Netherlands, but we could substitute Methodists or Baptists or Catholics or anything else — would participate without seeking hegemony over it. Part of his genius lay in seeing that such participation could not be done solely at the individual level, but called for distinctive institutions, institutions such as Christian colleges and universities, which would build and support communities. For society is not simply a collection of individuals held together by a state. Rather society is also composed of communities and institutions, entities larger than individuals and families but more concrete and real than the state in shaping the lives of human beings.

However, such institutions do not happen spontaneously. They are built by dedicated human beings, and they can only survive when they are intentionally cultivated and nourished. That is why the Christian scholar-teachers who are the heart and soul of Christian institutions of higher education must share a vision that is Kuyperian in spirit, a vision of a Christian faith that animates and shapes what we do as scholars and teachers.

Christian Calling: Authentic Christian Commitment

So my first point is the need for the Christian teacher-scholar to be committed to a vision of transformative Christianity. My second point, equally important, is that the Christian teacher-scholar has a specific calling and does his or her work in light of that calling. Søren Kierkegaard likes to describe a Christian as a person who tries to live his or her life as one who stands before God. As he puts it, the astounding thing about Christian faith is that each one of us, however unimportant we may feel ourselves to be, has the privilege of being personally addressed by God, the almighty one, the ruler of the universe. A person who might feel incredibly lucky to shake the hand of a presidential candidate in fact has a much more exalted status: he or she is called to live continually in the presence of God. And God has a unique name for each one of us, a unique set of tasks.

Wolterstorff has attempted to express a similar idea with the notion of "authentic Christian commitment."[3] He begins with the idea of a person's "*actual* Christian commitment," which is that "complex of action and belief" (I would add emotion) that commitment to Jesus of Nazareth has produced in that person.[4] The notion of "*authentic* Christian commitment" is a normative one. Given that "every Christian, whether liberal or conservative, has some notion of how his fundamental commitment ought to be realized," we can define authentic Christian commitment as "the complex of action and belief" that a given person's commitment to Jesus ought to manifest.[5]

This is obviously an ideal, but as an ideal it has a certain objectivity, and thus it is possible to be mistaken about what one's authentic Christian commitment demands. But it is also an ideal that is individualized and somewhat person-relative. I assume that what God wants from me is not exactly what God requires from you. What God expects of me today is not what he expected of me when I was fourteen years old. Some of what is called for by my authentic Christian commitment is shared in common with most other Christians. Some will be shared in common with other members of my particular church or denomination or theological tradition. Some will be unique to me because of my own particular situation or gifts.

The notion of authentic Christian commitment is a broad one. It cannot be identified with believing certain doctrines, though it will certainly make some difference to the beliefs I have. It cannot be identified with acting in a certain way, though it will certainly manifest itself in part through actions. It will also manifest itself in our emotional lives and the relationships we form, the institutions we participate in and the charac-

---

3. See Nicholas Wolterstorff, *Reason Within the Bounds of Religion* (Grand Rapids: Eerdmans, 1976), pp. 67-71.

4. Wolterstorff, *Reason Within the Bounds of Religion,* p. 68.

5. Wolterstorff, *Reason Within the Bounds of Religion,* p. 68.

ter of those institutions. Obviously, our authentic Christian commitment is far larger than our jobs. However, for the Christian it is crucial to see one's job and career as part of this calling or vocation. Whether I am cleaning toilets or searching for a cure for cancer, I should strive to see my work as work that God has called me to do, work that can be done for Christ's sake.

The calling of the Christian scholar-teacher is one that has particular relevance for both the church and the world in today's cultural situation. Part of this importance comes from the intrinsic importance of the mission of the Christian university: the Christian scholar-teacher is a person who believes deeply in the value of preparing students to become agents of the kingdom of God. In today's cultural situation there is a particularly strategic importance to this calling. Obviously, Christian professors are not necessarily better or more important than anyone else, but the role the Christian professor plays in society is strategically important.

In the church in which I grew up, we had annual missionary conferences, where the question was frequently posed: "Do you have a calling to the mission field?" As a child I felt that I did indeed have a calling to become a missionary. Yet I am now a professor of philosophy, definitely not what the speakers in the missionary conferences had in mind. Nonetheless, I am indeed a kind of missionary, and I certainly think that my work today is part of what God has called me to do.

I can remember very clearly the conversations I had when I was an undergraduate with Arthur Holmes, the professor at Wheaton College who was my mentor. Holmes told me clearly that I was called to be faithful, and that I must not worry about results, but leave them in God's hands. At the same time, he said that I had an obligation to think strategically about God's kingdom in the world today. Was it possible that God had some important work for me to do? Was there a place that I could invest my life strategically, a way to use the gifts and opportunities God had given me for his purposes? Though Holmes himself had a great vision (that God would use him to train a hundred Christians to work as Christian philosophers), the key question he posed was not "Will you become a philosopher?" but "How can you invest your life strategically for the kingdom of God?" Some of our students will indeed answer that question by choosing the career path of a teacher. But others will be called as pastors, physicians, lawyers, artists, musicians, engineers, or business people. Some will be called to public service, or to work with charitable organizations. Some will be called to foreign missions.

In any case, all of us who are Christ's disciples are missionaries of a sort. And specifically, all of us who are educated Christians have the opportunity to represent Christ to other members of our professions. We have the opportunity to employ our intellectual gifts and learning in the church and for the church. In fact, I would go so far as to say that the educated Christian is a kind of double missionary. On one hand the educated Christian is a representative of Christ's church in the spheres of life where intellectual issues are important, arenas that are culturally influential but where a Christian voice is often decidedly lacking. On the other hand, the Christian scholar is also a missionary for the life of the mind within the church, where as Mark Noll has written, "The scandal of the evangelical mind is that there is not much of an evangelical mind."[6] The Christian scholar has gifts of learning and insight to offer the church, and should see these gifts as valuable to the people of God.

So, to sum up so far, the calling of the Christian teacher-scholar forms the heart and soul of Christian higher education. The Christian professor must be committed to a transformative vision that allows him or her to work integrally and holistically within the academic world as a Christian. Seeking to be faithful to his or her authentic Christian commitment, the Christian professor is called to be a double missionary, representing the life of the mind within the church, and the life of the church to the intellectual world.

Such a conception of the Christian scholar leads logically to what George Marsden calls the outrageous idea of Christian scholarship.[7] But does the idea of Christian scholarship make sense? Is there such a thing as Christian mathematics or physics? Won't a Christian at work in the academic world who cares about truth and evidence come up with the same theories as a non-Christian?

6. Mark A. Noll, *The Scandal of the Evangelical Mind* (Grand Rapids: Eerdmans, 1994), p. 3.

7. George M. Marsden, *The Outrageous Idea of Christian Scholarship* (New York: Oxford University Press, 1997).

The Nature of Christian Scholarship

To answer these questions, let me begin with a definition: "Christian scholarship is scholarship that is done to further the kingdom of God. It is scholarship carried out as part of a *calling* by citizens of that kingdom whose character, attitudes, emotions, and convictions reflect their citizenship, and whose work as scholars is shaped by their Christian convictions, emotions, and character."[8]

Christian scholarship does not have to be or to appear uniquely or distinctively Christian. Often Christians are called to do the same experiments or construct the same mathematical proofs as non-Christians. One way that Christians may bear witness to the kingdom of God is simply by doing excellent work in their disciplines, contributing to the development of new knowledge, furthering the general good, and also demonstrating that it is possible for a thoughtful person to live as a Christian in today's world. This kind of scholarship may not be obviously Christian to an observer, but it is still scholarship that satisfies my definition of Christian scholarship, since the work is motivated by a desire to honor God. We could call it *purely vocational Christian scholarship.*

Sometimes, however, Christian scholarship will be different because of the Christian faith that lies at its heart. The differences will not always be explicit. David Myers, for example, a Christian psychologist at Hope College, has been doing research on the relationship between happiness and financial wealth. He is trying to show something that Christians know to be true, that mere wealth does not bring true satisfaction and happiness. His work is an instance of *implicit Christian scholarship* because while his Christian faith has shaped both his choice of the issue to be studied and the hypotheses he is testing, his research nevertheless is not overtly or explicitly Christian. Sometimes Christian faith makes a difference to scholarship without that difference being detectable. Of course I do not mean to suggest that the work Myers is doing could not have been done by a non-Christian. Obviously, that is possible. The point is that Myers's actual work is different than it would be if it were not being motivated and shaped by his Christian concerns.

8. Adapted from C. Stephen Evans, *Wisdom and Humanness in Psychology: Prospects for a Christian Approach* (Grand Rapids: Baker Book House, 1989), p. 132.

Christian faith shapes scholarly work in a more direct and obvious way in other cases. As an example I would cite my colleague John Hare and his recent book, *The Moral Gap*.[9] In this work Hare looks at modern moral philosophy, beginning with the great Enlightenment thinker Immanuel Kant, and tries to show that even within secular moral philosophy there is an awareness of a gap between what we humans recognize we should morally do and become, and what we are actually capable of doing and becoming. Hare points to this gap to argue for the continued relevance of the Christian claims that humans are in need of divine assistance — we need something like the atonement, a way of filling the moral gap, if we are to achieve our own moral ideals. He argues that the idea that Christ has made an atonement for us continues to make sense from the standpoint of moral philosophy. Hare's work, then, is *explicit Christian scholarship*. We might say it wears its Christian character on its sleeve, and is intended as a form of Christian apologetics and testimony.

Some Cautionary Thoughts

So what kind of Christian scholarship should we be doing — purely vocational, implicit, or explicit? All of the above, of course. Our callings reflect differences in our authentic Christian commitments, differences in what God expects from each of us. I shall say more later about the kinds of circumstances that may call for a particular form of Christian scholarship. For the moment I want to add some cautionary qualifications to what I have said about the need for Christian scholarship.

I want to emphasize that Christian scholarship is not monolithic but pluralistic, reflecting the diversity of Christians and their vocations. Christian scholars will not agree on everything, and that is not necessarily a bad thing. Thus, there is room within Christian scholarship for Christian feminism, Christian conservatism, Christian romanticism, etc. However, it is important to remember what is *absolute* and what is *relative,* what is ultimately important and what is only important.

Moreover, it must be emphasized that Christian scholarship can be done well or poorly. Christianity is no guarantee against shoddiness. The strongest argument against Christian scholarship is the shoddiness of

---

9. John E. Hare, *The Moral Gap: Kantian Ethics, Human Limits, and God's Assistance* (New York: Oxford University Press, 1997).

much of what claims to be Christian scholarship. Perhaps it is worth asking why so much of what represents itself as Christian thinking is simplistic or worse. Part of the answer lies in the ways we so often misuse Holy Scripture. The Bible is decisively important for Christian scholarship. But the Bible must be used properly. We cannot look to the Bible for quick fixes and prooftexts to answer every scholarly question. Protestants may be prone to this kind of simplistic use of the Bible due to the doctrine of the perspicuity of Scripture. This doctrine is an important part of the Protestant heritage, and is closely linked to the Baptist emphasis on the individual conscience of the believer struggling to understand the Bible. I do not wish to attack the doctrine of the perspicuity of Scripture itself. The "great things of the gospel" are clear and do not require great learning to be understood. However, it is often not clear how, and in fact it takes great effort to develop a Christian understanding of something such as sexuality or the family, and it takes great skill to apply Christian wisdom to contemporary problems and issues. It is true, as Kierkegaard says, that learning can sometimes be used to evade obedience; we would rather interpret God's word than act on it. However, on many issues biblical teachings are not clear and interpretation is genuinely complex.

Third, since Christians share in the finitude and sinfulness of the human race, Christian scholarship is fallible, and Christians often must learn from and be corrected by non-Christians. Christian scholarship cannot be done in an intellectual ghetto. Christians must be in dialogue and full communication with their non-Christian colleagues, not only to share their own insights, but also to learn from and build on what others have achieved.

Finally, Christian scholarship must be intellectually honest. The Christian scholar cannot and should not refuse to deal forthrightly with doubts and challenges. Though the romantic glorification of doubt should be avoided, doubt is part of our finitude and can itself be offered to God in prayerful devotion as in the prayer, "Lord, I believe. Help my unbelief." The Christian community must trust the community of Christian scholars and recognize the importance of academic freedom; in return the Christian scholar must affirm his or her ultimate loyalty to the church. A key role may be played here by the "friendly critic" or "friendly opponent" whose honest and open position can be more helpful than that of the insincere or reluctant adherent.

Seeing the World Through Biblical Eyes:
The Acts of the Drama

Christian faith is rooted in God's revelation in history and in the Bible. In some way the biblical revelation must be decisive in determining what our authentic Christian commitment demands of us. To understand how Christian scholarship that is implicitly or explicitly Christian might be different, we must understand how it is related to the Bible. The biblical revelation, as it is understood by the church, takes the form of a narrative — a story that is a grand drama with several important acts: creation, fall, redemption, sanctification, glorification, and final victory. I take it that what we call "doctrines" are attempts to articulate the meaning of some aspect of this narrative. Although theologians have a special responsibility to articulate these meanings, all followers of Christ must seek to understand this story and its meaning for their lives and the community of which they are a part. The story needs to become the "frame" or context in terms of which everything else is understood. What we need to develop is the habit of continually looking to Scripture to provide the basic or foundational narrative in terms of which we understand the world, rather than seeking easy answers to all of our questions.

We succumb to the challenge of "secularism" if we allow this narrative to be marginalized, because to become deeply Christian is to make this story the basic narrative that assigns meanings and values to all that one knows and experiences. Each element in the narrative can of course be articulated in different ways. Sometimes those differences reflect substantive disagreements; sometimes the disagreements reflect the richness and complexity of God's truth, which cannot be neatly packaged in human systems. As Christian scholars, we must continually seek to discern the relevance and power of the Christian narrative to illuminate the human condition, both universally and in our particular circumstances. What more, generally, might be said about this narrative?

Creation The debate about "creation science" and evolution has obscured the fundamental importance of this doctrine, which implies the fundamental goodness of the created order and the "creation mandate" to participate in that order. To believe in creation is not merely to believe that at some time in the past God started everything off and now things run on in their merry way. Rather, it is to believe that even now every aspect of nature depends on God and God's creative power. The world that God made is important because it is important to God. He is the one who made it and pronounced it good. If we value that creation and recognize its goodness, we will want to study it and know about it. A weak doctrine of creation is fatal to Christian higher education, and is the real root of the anti-intellectualism sometimes found in fundamentalism.

The status of human beings is a crucial element of the doctrine of creation. The biblical view of human creation contains a balanced tension between two emphases: humans are created from "dust" and yet are created in God's image. If we look at secular views of humanity, we can see how hard it is to maintain this balance. There is a tendency to err in one of two opposite directions: either we find *reductionism,* in which the uniqueness and significance of human life is undermined, or else *self-deification,* in which human beings are made the center of the universe, the source of all value and truth. The challenge to Christians is to hold together the tension between the recognition that we are creatures — dust — and the recognition that we have unique value and significance — as made in God's image.

Sin and the Fall   If fundamentalism is weak with respect to creation, liberalism is typically weak in its view of the fall and human sinfulness. Even if nothing else in Calvinism is acceptable, "total depravity," understood as the claim that every aspect of the created order is marred by sin, is the Christian doctrine best supported by experience. This has all kinds of implications. First of all, it means that Christians must always be concerned with their own motives, with the beams in their own eyes rather than the specks in their neighbors' eyes. It also means the conflict between faith and sin is not between "us and them" but within each one of us. As a Christian I see myself in a spiritual battle, but I dare not think of the battle as one that is waged against my non-Christian neighbor. We wrestle not against flesh and blood but against principalities and powers.

Incarnation and Redemption   Of course the most characteristic Christian conviction is the doctrine of the incarnation, the astounding claim that God himself has somehow become present with us in the form of a historical individual, Jesus of Nazareth. I agree with some medieval theologians that the incarnation would have occurred even if humans had not fallen. Even more than creation, the incarnation implies God's profound love for his creation and his continuing involvement with it. It is crucial that Christianity is a historical faith, and that it takes full account of the historical character of human life. Salvation is not a retreat to a world of timeless myth, but is an involvement with God in a contingent world, a world that is fallen but which God continues to love and seeks to redeem and restore. The incarnation, then, provides a kind of charter for engagement with the world, including scholarly engagement. The world, particularly the human world, is a world that God himself has become part of, and it therefore cannot be dismissed as unimportant. Whatever else Christianity may be, it cannot be a religion that focuses purely on the next life or the next world, since even the new life will be a resurrected life, a bodily life that will in some way be a fulfillment and continuation of this one.

Sanctification and Final Victory What does it mean to believe that Jesus Christ will return, that God will someday be totally victorious over evil? It means in part that the church is always in this life a church militant, never a church triumphant.[10] Nevertheless, however many defeats we suffer, however much evil may appear triumphant, we must live in the power of hope, a hope inspired by God's promise of final victory. We do not have the luxury of thinking that sin and suffering will finally have the upper hand; to think that way is to betray all those who have suffered evil and stood for righteousness.

The Impact of the Biblical Drama and the "Relevance Continuum"

If we really take this biblical drama as our basic narrative and frame of reference, will it make a difference to the way we do scholarship? The simple answer is, "Not always but sometimes." The complicated part is of course deciding when our scholarship should be different, even while we keep in mind that our vocation does not always require us to be dif-

---

10. The military metaphor reminds us that the church is locked in a battle not with human foes, but with spiritual forces.

ferent. We seek to be faithful, not to be different. However, if we are truly faithful, we will be different often enough.

I have said repeatedly that Christian scholarship does not have to be or appear to be uniquely or distinctively Christian either as product or process. We are often called to the same tasks as our non-Christian sisters and brothers. Nevertheless, if we are reflective and sensitive we can see that Christian faith may have an impact on any aspect of scholarship, from the choice of topics to investigate, to consideration of what counts as evidence, to thinking about how new knowledge should be used. Christianity may bear in a substantive manner on any academic discipline, though the frequency with which this occurs will vary from field to field and within a field according to the type of question being considered. The chart below illustrates this point by giving a sketch of what I call the "relevance continuum."

Relevance Continuum

(less)					(more)
<-->					
Mathematics	Natural Sciences	Human Sciences	History	Literature and the Arts	Philosophy and Theology

Although faith may have an impact on a question in any discipline, as one goes from the left to the right on this relevance continuum, this impact becomes much more common. The number of questions where faith will divide believers from nonbelievers is fewer as one goes to the left; the amount of common ground and the ease of finding it is smaller as one goes to the right, though it never vanishes altogether. Even in philosophy and theology there are many questions about which one's ultimate faith commitment will make no difference. One can also say that within a discipline, formal questions tend to be more neutral; however, as we approach ethical questions and questions that bear on basic worldviews, our disciplines become more value-charged. A few illustrations will be helpful in clarifying these points.

Most of us find the idea of a Christian mathematics slightly comical because so few of the questions that occupy a mathematician are substantively affected by the biblical narrative. A geometrical proof is a proof. Nevertheless, even in mathematics questions can be raised that are related to worldviews.[11] One of the most fundamental is the question as to the nature and status of numbers and other mathematical objects. Are numbers real? They do not seem to exist as spatiotemporal objects, but does this mean they do not exist at all? Is mathematical truth invented or discovered? Many mathematicians recognize that these questions are profoundly affected by our basic worldview. If we think that matter is all that is real and that human life is a cosmic accident, this may have a profound impact on how we see mathematics itself as a discipline. Ethical questions also present themselves as important ones that may be shaped by one's Christian convictions. One of the most striking aspects of mathematics is the way in which what appear to be esoteric discoveries eventually turn out to have practical applications. As soon as knowledge begins to be applied, we cannot avoid ethical questions about how it should be used.

The natural sciences are similar to mathematics in that the overwhelming majority of the questions pursued in everyday scientific work are not affected by the biblical framework. However, this is not true for all such questions. I know a philosopher of science who is doing a book on Michael Faraday, the famous chemist, in which he makes it clear that Faraday's Christian faith was one of the factors that inspired him to look for certain types of theories — theories that were eventually proved right — and reject others, even in the face of hostility from his scientific peers. As we go from day-to-day questions to more foundational questions in these disciplines, we once again see the effects of a biblical worldview or its lack. How, for example, should we view the orderliness of the scientific world itself? It does not seem necessary that our world should be governed by relatively simple laws, expressible in mathematical form and discoverable by human investigation. What does this orderliness and intelligibility suggest about our world? How should we view the whole question of the origin of the universe? Can science explain the Big Bang or does it inevitably point beyond itself? Motivated in part by these kinds of questions, the whole field of science and religion is booming at the moment, with a host of new research institutes and centers, and a great deal of research funded by the John Templeton Foundation.

As we move to the human sciences, the impact of the biblical narra-

11. See Russell W. Howell and W. James Bradley, *Mathematics in a Postmodern Age: A Christian Perspective* (Grand Rapids: Eerdmans, 2001).

tive becomes still greater. We can see the way Christian faith shapes scholarly work in this area if we look at how researchers choose the questions they want to pursue, define the basic concepts used in their research, and interpret and weigh evidence. If we want to study aggression, we have to decide when violence is justified, unprovoked, and defensive in nature and when it is not. If we want to study friendship, we need to decide how to define genuine friendship. If we want to study human happiness, we have to decide how to define and measure it.

A Christian psychologist, for example, might choose to study the topic of forgiveness because of the profound importance of forgiveness in the biblical drama. (I have a friend who is actually doing this; her preliminary results clearly show that a person who seeks to forgive another who has wronged her has lower blood pressure and heart rates than those who rehearse the wrongs or plot revenge.) But the impact of the biblical drama is not limited to choice of topic. Research findings must be interpreted and evidence must be weighed, and all of this may be shaped in subtle and not-so-subtle ways by worldview considerations. A Christian psychologist, for example, will be inclined to be skeptical about research that purports to show that humans are incapable of genuine love for another.

The situation of history is somewhat similar to the human sciences. I have a friend, Dale Van Kley, who is a Christian historian and who has spent a lifetime studying the causes of the French Revolution. When he began his career, the French Revolution was generally viewed in Marxist terms as an outgrowth of economic class conflict. Van Kley, as a Christian scholar, was convinced that the Marxist view of human history was too simple. Moral and religious beliefs cannot be mere epiphenomena to be explained by underlying economic factors. After thirty years of research he has developed solid historical evidence that religious beliefs and conflicts actually played an important role in the development of the French Revolution.

It is even easier to show the impact of worldviews in such areas as literature, the arts, philosophy, and theology. I am convinced, for example, that the great monotheistic faiths provide a basis for human equality that is superior to any that has been proposed by secular moral philosophers. If we believe that all human persons are made in God's image, then we have a reason to think that all human persons have intrinsic value and should never be regarded purely as means to other ends. We rightly ask why there are so many religious conflicts in our world, and are horrified by the thought of ethnic cleansing. But we should ask why ethnic cleansing is indeed horrifying, for to many human cultures it has seemed self-evident that it was acceptable for one culture, tribe, or clan to exterminate its neighbors. So in these areas, questions of meaning and value often lie at the very center of our work.

Still, we must be reminded that not every question even in these fields will be influenced by faith. An argument about an author's grammatical proclivities that depends on a word-frequency count provides the same evidence for Christians and non-Christians. The vividness of a color may be the same for both. The formal validity of a logical argument in philosophy is the same for everyone who considers the matter. Common ground and persuasive arguments can often be found. But not always.

Is Christian Scholarship Really Scholarship?

I can imagine an objection at this point that might go like this: "I acknowledge the sad truth that our scholarship is often affected by our religious views, and perhaps by our secular worldviews as well. However, that is regrettable and simply shows that we have not been rigorous enough in doing our scholarship. If we are truly intellectually honest, we will approach all questions in a completely objective manner and simply look for the truth, letting the chips fall where they may." Can scholarship be Christian without undermining its character as scholarship?

This challenge raises questions about the relation of Christian scholarship to what has become known as postmodernism. Can we acknowledge that scholarship can be shaped by a worldview such as Christianity without succumbing to relativism and the despairing view of the intellectual life that sees all academic work as essentially political power fights? If Christians do their scholarly work as Christians, motivated by what I called the transformative vision and a sense of vocation, will their scholarship be reduced to partisanship, ideology, or even propaganda? To answer these questions, we must think hard about what has come to be known as the postmodern academic situation and the place of Christians in today's academic world.

Some Christian thinkers have argued that the postmodern rejection of "classical foundationalism" and recognition of the situated character of human reason opens the door for greater Christian participation in the academy. On this view, the modernist view that arose at the time of the Enlightenment is one that tried to shut religious perspectives out of the academy and other public human endeavors. Reacting to the religious wars of the post-Reformation era, they thought that the way to reach truth was to seek for knowledge in a neutral, detached way. We might say that they wanted to raise over the gates of the university a large inscription: "All who wish to enter here must shed their human particularities, especially religious particularities, and seek to become generically rational beings." Those who want to enter the scholarly path must then put aside religious and moral convictions and try to see the world from a godlike point of view.

Postmodernism can be seen, in part, as the recognition that we do not and cannot occupy such a point of view. The postmodernist says that it can and sometimes does make a difference to our thinking if we are male or female, white or black, gay or straight, European or Asian. In *The Outrageous Idea of Christian Scholarship,* Marsden argues that this new situation is favorable to a Christian presence in the academy. It makes it possible for engaged Christian scholars, as well as Jewish, Islamic, Hindu, and Buddhist scholars, to claim a seat at the academic table and seek to be part of a pluralistic conversation, without having to shed their religious identity.

Other Christian scholars see more threat than opportunity to Christian faith in a postmodern academic world. As they see things, many postmodernists embrace a relativistic view of the world that undermines a concern for objective truth and leads only to the politicizing of the academy. On this view a postmodern academy has given up on truth altogether and focuses only on questions of oppression and victimization. Another problem with postmodernism, as such critics see the situation, is that it rejects the possibility of what is called a "meta-story," an overarching narrative regarded as truth that is supposed to give meaning and structure to the whole of human experience. Surely, the great biblical drama that I discussed above is supposed to function as such a meta-story for Christians.

So who is right? Is modernity a villain or part of our Christian heritage? Is postmodernism our salvation or does it lead to perdition? The answer, I think, is a prosaic and unexciting one: "Both modernity and postmodernity have insights that the Christian can appropriate. Neither can be wholeheartedly accepted." The above issues provide a dramatic example of the importance of nuance for the Christian scholar, who must not give in to the temptation to embrace or reject uncritically either the "modern" or the "postmodern." There are elements in modernity that Christianity must criticize; to the degree that postmodernism opens up the possibility of such a critique it is a welcome development.

However, the Christian must not throw the baby out with the bathwater. In questioning the supposed godlike objectivity of the human mind, we must not throw out the possibility that there is a truth that we can approximate and should seek to approximate. In recognizing that we are concerned and committed beings, and that our ideas have implications, including social and political ones, we must not give up on the values of honesty and concern for truth. We have a meta-story, and are committed to the claim that this story, the story of creation, fall, redemption, and final victory, is not merely a private story, but the story of the God of the entire universe. However, we must always remember that this grand story is indeed grand; it is God's story and it is always grander than any particular human version of the story. It is, in fact, to this story that we must turn to illumine our path. In doing so, we will find that the great biblical drama, the grand Christian narrative, contains resources for navigating the tricky waters of contemporary academia.

Our challenge is to understand and accept our historical situation without despairing over the possibility of progress towards truth. This task is mirrored by our responsibility to help students acquire both humility and conviction. It is not easy to teach our students to be modest and cautious, to help them see the complexity of many issues and the possibility of mistakes, and at the same time to develop passionate commitments. Yet I think that this is what we want to accomplish. We want them to see and understand the problems and difficulties, to be able to see the world through the eyes of those who disagree with them. Yet we also want them to have the courage of their convictions, to combine intellectual humility with the courage and passion of the martyr.

What does this mean, practically, for the Christian academic today? Should we seek to follow the tide of postmodernism and argue, as Marsden has done, that if feminist scholarship, gay and lesbian scholarship, and Marxist scholarship are legitimate, then Christian scholarship is legitimate as well? We can cautiously embrace Marsden's proposal and hold the academic community to its word when it says it wants a pluralistic conversation. We can rightly ask for a seat at the table. Nevertheless, we should not have to accept assumptions of methodological atheism or relativism to be part of a conversation that is genuinely open to the other. My proposal means Christians must be serious about pluralism. We must not seek to recreate medieval Europe or seek to recreate a mythical Christian America that never really existed. The age of Constantine and Constantinian Christianity is over.

However, on balance the end of Constantinian Christianity is a good thing. Christianity always gets into trouble when it becomes too closely identified with a particular human culture. This is one insight that Baptist distinctives have helped to safeguard. The defense of believer's baptism is in part a defense of the important truth that one does not become a Christian simply by virtue of being born into a Christian culture or a Christian family. To be a Christian one must be born again. But if a person confuses becoming a Christian with being born the first time, it is hard to see the necessity for a second birth. The temptation in such a case is always to confuse Christian nurture with acculturation. Christian faith must always be expressed in and through human culture, but it must never be identified with any particular human culture. In fact, it is in many ways a blessing and perhaps part of the providence of God that the center of dynamic Christian faith seems to be shifting from Europe and North America to Africa and Asia. This should make it clear that Christianity is not simply a Western religion, even if it has left its mark on various dimensions of Western culture. Christianity is, more than ever, a world religion, and its ability to adapt itself to and express itself in very different cultures is amazing and powerful. But it can only do so by refusing to identify itself with any of its particular cultural expressions.

The Christian, I am suggesting, is not merely a grudging pluralist, who settles for a weak voice since Christianity can no longer control the culture. Rather, the Christian is a principled pluralist, who recognizes that to be a Christian is always to stand in tension with what the Bible calls the world. We must be content to rest in the power of words and the Word; we are most successful when we rely on the power of loving example. We are content to be one voice in a larger conversation, not because we think all voices are equally right, but because we have confidence in the power of God's Spirit. We are convinced that God has spoken and we want to be witnesses to God's word. However, we know we have an obligation to hear as well as speak, and that the God who can speak through Balaam's ass can speak through the voices of all his created children, can speak to us as well as through us.

The Christian must be a pluralist, therefore, not because that is all we can manage in a fractured, postmodern world, but because that is what our faith itself demands from us. We follow the crucified one, who, though himself innocent, conquered evil through a willingness to suffer at the hands of injustice. Those who follow Jesus should not seek to achieve their aims through any kind of coercion or violence. A stance of tolerance and respect is well suited to a faith that holds that not even God is willing to coerce true faith, but attempts to woo a rebellious world by an act of loving sacrifice.

Kierkegaard in one of his books compares the story of the incarnation to a fairy tale in which a powerful king falls in love with a simple peasant maid. How can the king woo his love? He could simply order her to be his wife and threaten her with the dungeon if she refuses. But such a forced response could never satisfy a loving heart. He could dazzle her with the splendors of his palace and his riches, but then he might worry that she cared for these things more than himself. No, the king must woo his love by coming to her in disguise, by presenting himself as a peasant like her.

And so with the incarnation, though in this case God does not adopt a mere disguise. He does not merely present himself as human, but actually enters our world and assumes our condition. For only in this way could we understand how deep and powerful is his love for us, and respond with love of our own that is free and uncoerced. As followers of this incarnate God, we can be no less respectful of the freedom and integrity of those we seek to win. In a pluralistic community Christians must model respect and tolerance, even while they show that intellectual humility can coexist with committed conviction and action. The church can seek to transform the world without seeking to use worldly means that rely on power and manipulation. In this way, we live up to our noble calling as Christian scholar-teachers, furthering the kingdom of God through our work and lives.

QUESTIONS FOR REFLECTION AND DISCUSSION

1. Evans proposes a Kuyperian-inspired "transformative Christian vision," a vision of a pluralistic society in which Christians participate

without seeking hegemony over it. It is this vision, he suggests, that ought to motivate the work of Christian scholar-teachers. What difficulties, if any, are there to realizing this vision, whether from the perspective of Christian faith and life or that of the wider culture?

2. Given Evans's claim that the calling of the Christian scholar-teacher forms the heart and soul of Christian higher education, how might that calling be affirmed and deepened among those already in the profession? How might that calling be heard, affirmed, or deepened among students on whom the future of Christian higher education depends?

3. Distinctions among purely vocational Christian scholarship, implicit Christian scholarship, and explicit Christian scholarship — as well as Evans's cautionary thoughts — help make sense of varied forms of good Christian scholarship. How would you describe your own scholarly efforts? How might Evans's distinctions guide your ongoing or future research projects? What implications do these distinctions have for pedagogy?

4. Regarding the grand biblical drama, Evans writes, "To become deeply Christian is to make this story the basic narrative that assigns meanings and values to all that one knows and experiences." Various acts of the drama might shape one's discipline in important ways. For the natural sciences, the doctrine of creation conveys the original and ultimate orderliness, beauty, and intelligibility of the cosmos. For the social sciences, creation and fall together imply both the possibility of civilization and the probability of conflict and war. For the arts, creation suggests that the source of our creative impulse comes from the Creator-God in whose image we are, and that in the character of God may be discovered the standards of beauty by which we should judge our artistic productions. Keeping in mind Evans's caution that developing an informed, nuanced Christian understanding of such matters is not a simple matter, what implications for your discipline seem to follow from taking the Christian narrative in all its aspects seriously?

5. What is Evans's response to the challenge of postmodernism? How would partisans of either modernist or postmodernist inclination respond to his "prosaic" answer?

FURTHER RELATED WORK BY THIS AUTHOR

Evans, C. Stephen. *Philosophy of Religion: Thinking About Faith*. Downers Grove, Ill.: InterVarsity Press, 1985.

——. *Wisdom and Humanness in Psychology: Prospects for a Christian Approach*. Grand Rapids: Baker, 1989.

——. *The Historical Christ and the Jesus of Faith: The Incarnational Narrative as History*. New York: Oxford University Press, 1996.

——. *Why Believe? Reason and Mystery as Pointers to God*. Grand Rapids: Eerdmans, 1997.

Chapter Three

The Church and Christian Higher Education in the New Millennium

MARTIN E. MARTY

Question: *Exactly, precisely* what do I hope to achieve on these pages? Answer: I hope that I can contribute to a conversation among Christian college and university educators that will help provide part of the framework for their common work in the years ahead.

Phrasing it in this way makes it possible to rule out several topics that form a penumbra or have tentacular relations to this. Thus, we will not go into questions of denominational or other ministries in higher education, for example through worshiping communities at state universities or merely private colleges. At the same time, I hope what is written here will be of interest both to colleges and universities that are structurally related to various denominations as well as to those that have loose or no formal ties at all, but that want to affirm their Christian heritage. There may be some glancing remarks tilted toward Christian academies, even if they consider themselves to be half-higher education. I hope that something said here might interest people in theological schools, but the main concern here is not with the formal preparation of people for professional ministry. (Except, that is, in cases where colleges and universities prepare graduates for youth, education, music, and

---

This chapter was presented as an H. I. Hester Lecture at the June 4-7, 2000, meeting of the ASBCS, and adapted for this collection from the Third Quarter 2000 issue of *The Southern Baptist Educator.*

other ministries for which theological school preparation is not required or a *desideratum*.) Finally, there is no burden here for us to engage the question of religious studies.

There is a bit more delimiting to do. The word "millennium" appeared in the title because it was part of the assignment. But I know that the assigners were not preoccupied with the turning of a particular year for intrinsic, eschatological, or apocalyptic reasons. I picture them using the calendar-page turn as the occasion to live out the meaning of the biblical text, "Teach us to number our days, that we may apply our hearts unto wisdom" (Ps. 90:12). Thus, there is no reason for me to predict or foresee the future. I recall Yogi Berra's word, "It is very difficult to predict — especially if it's about the future!" Instead, the historian in me tells me to use the approach of Abraham Lincoln to the past: "If we could first know where we are, and whither we are tending, we could then better judge what to do, and how to do it."[1] So I shall describe some "where and whither" themes for others to develop on "what to do and how to do it."

My vantage? I share concern from within for church, Christianity, education, and the times in which we live. Second, I inhabit the same pluralist, diverse society in which Christian higher education makes its way. Finally, I am aware that different parts of the church have different understandings of the intellectual life, character formation, community, biblical interpretation, doctrine, and church-relation. Thus, Lutherans like myself stand somewhere between the writings out of Catholicism by Father James Burtchaell and those out of a Reformed influence by George Marsden and the like. So, from this vantage, what should be said about the church and Christian higher education in the new millennium?

All Things Hold Together in Christ

Colossians 1:15-20 provides a biblical text that well constitutes a fundamental charter for church-related higher education:

1. Abraham Lincoln, "A House Divided," in *The Collected Works of Abraham Lincoln*, vol. 2, ed. Roy P. Basler (Springfield, Ill.: The Abraham Lincoln Association, 1959), p. 461.

Christ is the image of the invisible God; his is the primacy over all created things. In him everything in heaven and on earth was created, not only things visible but also the invisible orders of thrones, sovereignties, authorities, and powers; the whole universe has been created through him and for him. And he exists before everything, and all things are held together in him. He is, moreover, the head of the body, the church. . . . For in him the complete being of God, by God's own choice, came to dwell. Through him God chose to reconcile the whole universe to himself, making peace through the shedding of his blood upon the cross — to reconcile all things, whether on earth or in heaven, through him alone.

There are strong temptations to exegete this passage and to study its context — and then go home. Had the Colossians planned a church-related university, they would have had many of the issues we have two millennia later. There were doctrinal disputes, factionalisms, fusions of Christian with pagan and maverick Jewish forces. In the face of all this it was important for Paul to stress that Jesus was prime and supreme. Picture a modern megabookstore being at home there, with its wall marked: "Religion, Spirituality, Wholistic, Holistic, Alternative Medicine, New Age, Ancient, Occult, Metaphysical, Astrology, Self-Help, Inspiration."

Where does this text fit into my own long interest in our subject? Around 1970, when the hippie and dissent era were beginning to end and the New Religions were emerging, there were cultural heirs of all of the above who were "Jesus People," ready to make a mark. They chose to make one of their splats on my personal windshield, as follows.

The Earl Lectures of the Pacific School of Religion are given in the large sanctuary of First Congregational Church in Berkeley, which can host a larger audience than can the nearby theological schools. I shared the platform for three-plus-three talks with Professor Robert McAfee Brown. After our evening duo we found that stage filling with what looked like a group of Hell's Angels, except they had short hair, were clean shaven, and relatively courteous. What did they want? While Brown and I twiddled thumbs and shifted foot-to-foot, our hosts did the discerning and the negotiating. It turns out that our visitors were "Jesus People," ex- of Campus Crusade, I believe. They had some name (the World Christian Liberation Front comes to mind), and a banner with that year's Jesus People slogan — an arrow with the words "One Way" on it. They asked for equal time, which turned out to be fifteen minutes. While they spaced themselves precisely on the stage, one of the twelve, a science professor, made a little speech.

The gist: Brown and I had spoken as professors. Guilty, as charged; professors we were, and professors tend to talk like professors. Guilty of what? Of quoting all kinds of living, non-biblical authors and books. They said that they were people of The One Book, and for the present cultural crisis Christian intellectuals should forego encounter with any other books or ideas not clearly contained in their Military Manual, the Bible. I asked them on what grounds they came to this parsimonious and spare Christian interpretation of the intellectual and moral life? The Bible. Who was their favorite author in it? Paul the apostle, said the spokesperson.

Out came my Ivy League-svelte thin New Testament, to Colossians 1. I had them read this passage. Now, *if* it is true that "everything in heaven and earth was created" and "all things are held together in him," was it not important to understand something about that to which he was and is related? Yes. "Everything?" That included:

a. the curricula of the Graduate Theological Union and our host, the Pacific School of Religion;
b. the libraries of the neighborhood, all books in them, all that is in all the books;
c. the San Francisco area phone book and the rosters of student housing and faculty members;
d. the ideas generated by all the above.

Being interested and understanding, of course, did not mean affirming all that was in all. That would have been impossible, because there might be six inner contradictions per paragraph, and we must assume that all the people implied were sinners. But Christians could not *not* be engaged with what all this represented. Neither we nor the group "won" that night, though I think we all listened to each other, and the audience found reason to affirm our continuing in the third day of lectures. I do not know what became of the WCLF (or whatever), though I am told some of them are now communicants and leaders in branches of the Eastern Orthodox Church, which also affirms Paul's Christ and relates to "everything," together with the notion of discerning what it means that all things "hold together" in Christ.

If you find anything to affirm in that encounter, its aftermath, and my proposal about what that means for today, we are poised to charter Christian higher education, with all its complications. We do so in an environment somewhat similar to that at Colossae in Paul's days. This means that it is secular, pluralist, spiritual, religious, and partly Christian.

Let me propose a thesis that is beginning to grow out of the scene just described. This work of Christian higher education in church-related institutions occurs at the juncture of several sets of entities or descripts that we used to think of as opposites, antagonisms — but today, for good reasons and bad, and with both promise and threat, these zones tend to blur, fuse, overlap, and lose their distinctiveness. I have in mind tensions between the material and the spiritual, the secular and the religious, the privileged and the exposed, and vocation and Vocation.

The Material and the Spiritual

We all know to think of the "invisible orders of thrones, sovereignties, authorities, and powers" of which Paul writes as being "spiritual," usually in their negative potency. Similarly, many Christians think that the positive counterparts to each of these, the "spiritual," make up the agenda and zone of concern for Christians. This would mean the winning and care of souls; keeping an eye on eternity; spreading the works of consolation; in general, doing the very, very, but not exclusively important things the church does and should do. There is no reason to pull back from commitment to any of that, but you do not need higher education to promote such concentrations.

However, it is important to notice and, with caution, to affirm the material order in which higher educators and their students and supporters find themselves. We do that all the time, but sometimes grudgingly, guiltily, or subvertly. It is important to arrange every aspect of higher education in ways that show a concern for the material order. For one instance, this means not to be afraid of money. The college and university presidents and development officers know this, because they know that survival is at stake. Some faculty members and supporters shuffle and mumble when material things get brought up, except at times of tenure and salary decisions. Nevertheless, material resources

54

are important. Survival may not be the noblest thing we do, but a friend reminds me that "if we don't survive, we don't do anything else, either."

What you are reading is a plug for bold, unabashed promotion of stewardship, for the sake of the hearts and minds of the stewards. We have moved into a whole new cultural stage, and many of our church members share dimensions of affluence undreamed of years ago. Their support of Christian education, not necessarily through their congregations but as individuals, alumni and alumnae groups, support clubs, and representation to fiscal elites, has not increased proportionately with their giving potential. Support for the academy is on the short end of things. A whole new generation has come to a place where it can give a high priority to colleges and universities, and we have to train them to build for the longer future. We can do all the evangelizing and converting we would like — never enough, to be sure — but if we "land" people on shores where they meet unchallenged secular lures they will not build on the reality of Christ "in whom all things hold together."

Beyond working for better resources that will assure futures well into the new millennium, there are other aspects of the material beyond stewardship where spiritual concerns arise. I assume that our own students are like most others in at least one respect: while many of them pursue vocations and professions that will not assure a rich material future, most of them are *en route* to places in our market economy. This economy assures that four-fifths of our citizens will share abundance undreamed of in previous cultures, including our own antecedency.

If our schools are "secularizing," they are doing so not because a secular humanist conspiracy or a group of Supreme Court or theologically liberal subversives are leading in that direction. They are doing so unthinkingly, by adopting the material norms of a market economy. They enter a world of consumerism. I see no Christian reason to wish our way out of abundance into want, though I am aware that participation in our "way" leads many to lose empathy for the dispossessed, whose way of life most of our grandparents shared. It may lead to unresponsiveness, judgmentalism, pride, and selfishness — *but it does not have to.* Indeed, Christian higher education exists in part not to get students out of the material world. Someone has said that Christianity itself is a very material religion: you can't even get it started without material things like a loaf of bread, a bottle of wine, and a river. Jesus was incarnate in our material world. He was hanged on a material cross, and though he preached against storing our treasures only among material things that rust, he also enjoyed banquets and did not turn his back on all the wealthy.

What we lack, says a University of Chicago colleague of mine who celebrates the market triumph, is even the beginning of personal and social philosophies through which to interpret and "redeem" and transform the material world of abundance. I do not think that the state university has in its charter much of a concern to help formulate instruments for interpretation. I do not want to make that claim too exclusive or emphatic; some philosophers, economists, and ethicists not of faith communities are serious contributors, but Christians have special, transcendental, eye-on-eternal reasons for going deeper and coming up with skeins of coherence in Christ.

To survive we often convert our schools from liberal arts with professional outreach to almost nothing-but-professional (e.g., business skills) reach. What are the terms on which we reason and frame alternatives within the material order? We should see church-related higher educators making a difference here, at least in the lives we touch. Do we?

As for the "spiritual" side, this fuses too easily with the material; hence the old spiritual/material dialectic does not hold well. The Christian faith has spiritual dimensions, but it celebrates the living God, the divine Person or Being incarnate in the man Christ Jesus. It has religious dimensions, and finds abodes in institutions, organizations, and academies. But today it makes its claims in a world in which different "spiritualities" make their claim and produce times and places that make us look like first-century Colossae. Thus, spirituality today often refers to something that is innate in the human soul, not interrupted by divine intervention; a belief in "the god within you," and in "connections" and "energy" more than in the Connector and Creator of the energy. Christian educators cannot simply sit back and enjoy the moments when the megabookstore, the celebrity, the therapist, and the generalizers and universalizers say something "spiritual" and then consider our job half done. Today's spirituality needs judgment, for too much a part of it are invisible thrones, sovereignties, authorities, and powers.

In our time Christians such as Martin Luther King, Jr., Mother Teresa, Dag Hammarskjold, Dietrich Bonhoeffer, and others have shown that the way of spirituality is also the way of action, of agency, of making a difference in God's world, while drawing on and contributing to the rich spiritual trove of the church. Students are not going to learn that from movies, MTV, or most uses of the Internet, any more than they will get it in chapel at most tax-supported institutions. Do they "learn that" in church-related centers of education?

The Secular and the Religious

With good reason the Burtchaells, Marsdens, and lesser folk decry secularism and secularization in higher education. But today the secular order does not come in a neat and self-enclosed package on its side of walls of separation. The secular refers to "the present age." It need not be a sphere of militant anti-religion or anti-Christianity. In fact, the secular today is more of an open system, more ready to be seen as overlapping the sphere of the religious. Certainly we inherit the legacy of secularizing forces: the Renaissance, the Enlightenment, Modernity. We have come to recognize the mixed blessings from these, like increases in freedom, autonomy, liberating criticism, and celebration of human creativity and construction. But when "autonomy" gets grounded in the autonomous, as in "I'll do it my way," and becomes divorced from its rootage in divine Being, the secular drift makes its way without needing to be dependent on anything militant.

To be clear, then, secularization comes less from the heirs of Darwin, Nietzsche, Marx, Freud, and the other bearded God-killers, or from clean-shaven federal bureaucrats, than from "everydayishness" of sorts students will not recognize unless our religious institutions provide means for teaching discernment. This subtle secularization poses a real risk. For wittingly or unwittingly, explicitly or implicitly, it leads to habits of mind and hand that suggest that the human project can be brought off and the human prospect fulfilled without any reference to any "beyond," anything not merely pragmatic and empirical, anything transcendental or revelational, or, in our context, where all things cohere in Christ.

There is also, however, a positive secularity that the stage-storming Liberation Front did not yet have room for. Another Pauline text says that "all things are yours . . . and you are Christ's and Christ is God" (1 Cor. 3:21-23), another charter for awareness of "all things." Don't we include chemistry, physical education, French, and philosophy in that? Are our schools helping prepare Christian young people to penetrate the worlds of politics and entertainment? The question does not answer it-self: no doubt some are. But if we want to know "whither we are tend-ing" we will learn to include these in our scope as never before.

As for the religious side of this polarity, where the poles are brought together, this distinction has become smudged — there too are negative and positive dimensions. I sometimes watch Christians and others plug-ging for "religion in the public square," meaning in public schools and court house lawns or walls, in the form of prayer and devotion and carved images of commandments, as if religion as such is better than non-religion as such. Not necessarily, as a generation or two of theologians re-minded us. Karl Barth had a chapter *Religion als Unglaube,* religion as unfaith.[2] He was aware that people can use private and public religious constructs to kid themselves that they do not need the gospel. Things can "hold together" in religion apart from Christ; but our search is for the co-herence Christ brings, in the religious dimensions of higher education.

There is also a positive side. No matter what the whiners say about the decline of religion in the public sphere, we can document an increas-ing interest in religion — not just "spirituality" — in artistic, entertain-ment, political, educational, and many other spheres. This presence cre-ates openings in which Christians can bring up subjects and stress emphases that they could not in a "merely" and "unblurred" secular en-vironment. A slogan of our Public Religion Project was "No Whining!" No one changes positively because whining goes on. (Peter Berger used to talk about how Christians bewailed secularity and told everyone to avoid the secular, and then bemoaned the reality of a secular society. That is like blond parents blaming their daughter for being blond: they produced her!) People change because someone offers them instru-ments and rationales for change. Higher education that coheres in Christ can help bring about change.

The Privileged and the Exposed

A third zone in which blurring is occurring where there had been sharp opposition or drastic polarity in higher education has to do with what I

2. Karl Barth, *Church Dogmatics* I/2, ed. G. W. Bromiley and T. F. Torrance (Edin-burgh: T. & T. Clark, 1936-1977), pp. 297-325.

call "privileged" and "privileging" contexts, readings, and proposals. Time was when Christian institutions of higher education were conceived as a kind of greenhouse. Within, "privileged" people, i.e., people who "read together privately" — which is partly what "privileged" means — did all that they could to keep out the winds of change, the breezes of the exotic, the climates of "out there." All they were supposed to do was to shelter against hurricanes and sudden freezes. As such, while fearing unsheltered exposure to atheist assumptions in arts and sciences, Christian educators warded off all expressions of the very cultures in which their graduates must live and move and have their being. They did them a disservice.

Meanwhile, at the other extreme, another set of Christian educators knocked out all the panes, broke the thermostats, and let all the winds of modernity and secularity blow through, until nothing was left about which to be distinctive. They "gave the game away," as Burtchaell, Marsden, and others have eloquently shown.

Instead, picture church-related higher education as still somewhat sheltered, privileging some "readings," but — if it can be represented as a greenhouse — also aware that the door does not always close, the panes are not all thermally sealed, and the thermostat is not completely sure — and that's all right. For that means that students will be dealing with the world in which coherence in Christ is not apparent, and must be ascertained, striven for, and then accepted as a gospel gift.

In such a setting students will read other than Christian and often anti-Christian texts, but will read them with a difference as they learn what to affirm and what to negate in them. By contrast, they will not at State U. get these mingled with audacious Christian texts such as the Bible and great Christian literature or scientific proposals. I overheard a friend who was asked why she chose to teach literature at an evangelical school when other institutions were open to a person of her accomplishment. "Because in such a school," she said, "we do not have to stop when we get to the deep things. We can plunge into them." Deep things: the World Christian Liberation Front's Bible and the forbidding Berkeley curriculum *both, and at the same time.* That is what I mean by a new understanding of what "privileging" means in church-related higher education.

"vocation" and "Vocation"

I want to add one more juncture at which Christian higher education occurs. I think that church-related higher educational institutions have to be *vocational* schools while they are *Vocational* schools. That is, while we must prepare students for vocations — more urgently than we prepare them for professions, careers, or jobs — we do not disdain the practical skills that go with vocations as usually understood. Anyone with a few funds and teachers can do the latter kind of practical vocational training. However, only Christian higher education is committed to what Christians mean by *Vocation*. They mean lives that find their coherence in Christ, "in whom everything holds together." They learn that each of them is distinctively marked, irreplaceable, in God's scheme of things, and that they are not merely integers among the thrones and principalities and authorities.

For this task we seek to build community in church-related higher education, to develop character with the special Christian stamp. No one has to come to church-related schools to get vocational training. They can probably get it as well or better elsewhere. But everyone who becomes part of Christian higher education should be confronted with, challenged by, and lured to Vocational training, a calling under God, in Christ.

How each school and each part of each school should contribute to this distinctive task will be up to each school, which has its own genius. If they undertake this in the world of lessened polarities and greater blurs between spheres and among zones, they will have located something truly distinctive, and worth pursuing, millennium long.

QUESTIONS FOR REFLECTION AND DISCUSSION

1. Marty aspires to describe "where we are, and whither we are tending." Where, on his view, does the Christian academy find itself today? Given this context and Christian confessional commitments, whither should it tend?
2. Christian higher education, Marty writes, occurs "at the juncture of several sets of entities or descripts that we used to think of as opposites, antagonisms — but today, for good reasons and bad, and with both promise and threat, these zones tend to blur, fuse, overlap, and

lose their distinctiveness." As evidence, he discusses would-be po-larities like the material and the spiritual, the secular and the reli-gious, the privileged and the exposed, and vocation and Vocation. What promises and threats attend the blurring of these aspects of life? Why is the Christian college or university an apt place to engage such questions?

3. Marty seeks to understand our present context and our ultimate aims for the sake of clarifying "what to do, and how to do it." How-ever, he does not venture far into offering programmatic recom-mendations. In light of the issues he raises, what is there to be done within your own teaching, scholarly endeavor, department or col-lege curriculum, and so on? How will it be done?

FURTHER RELATED WORK BY THIS AUTHOR

Marty, Martin E. *Education, Religion, and the Common Good: Advancing a Dis-tinctly American Conversation About Religion's Role in Our Shared Life.* San Francisco: Jossey-Bass, 2000.

Chapter Four

The Mission of Christian Scholarship in the New Millennium

JOEL A. CARPENTER

There are many challenges facing Christian scholarship, and I am tempted to give a survey of the front. I am going to resist that urge, however, in order to focus on one of the greatest challenges that Christian scholars face going forward: keeping a clear vision of what we are trying to accomplish. What is the mission of Christian scholarship? What are we trying to do? Without clarity of purpose, this enterprise will founder. If our mission is not compelling, the churches, upon which we rely for spiritual strength, institutional support, and accountability, will cut us loose. Without a singular vision, we will become distracted by the myriad issues swirling about the academy and be fully assimilated into its governing values and outlook. I want to focus on our mission. Before diving right into that subject, however, I do want to lay out a bit of context, speaking first about the current status of Christian scholarship, then about the current ideological atmosphere in the academy, and then finally and most importantly about our mission, and how it relates to the great mission of the church of Jesus Christ.

This chapter was presented as an H. I. Hester Lecture at the June 4-7, 2000, meeting of the ASBCS, and adapted for this collection from the Fourth Quarter 2000 issue of *The Southern Baptist Educator.*

A Time to Be Encouraged

It is an exciting time to be engaged in scholarly work as a Christian, even though the American academy is not much more favorable to the integration of faith and scholarship than it was a decade ago. Most academics, who are secular in outlook and allegiance, find the very idea of integrally Christian scholarship to be something like weird science. Bringing one's religious faith to bear on the assumptions, methodologies, and structures that govern academic work is rather risky, especially if one's faith is traditional Christianity. Nevertheless, I detect a growing desire among Christians in the academy to pursue their calling in integrally Christian ways. It is encouraging to see study centers springing up to foster such work, such as the Erasmus Institute at the University of Notre Dame, the Center for Law and Religion at Emory University, and the Institute for Faith and Learning at Baylor University.

There is also at least a modicum of interest on the American intellectual scene as to what these Christian scholars are doing. Alan Wolfe, a political science professor at Boston College, has been leading the way in acquainting secular intellectuals with the rise of Christian scholarship in recent years. Wolfe reviewed both of George Marsden's recent books on Christianity's role in the American academy. In his review of *The Soul of the American University* (1994) for *Lingua Franca* in 1996, Wolfe argued against giving a welcome to religious ideas in scholarly discourse. Religion is too disruptive, he thought, to add anything positive to the conversation. A year later, when he reviewed Marsden's next book, *The Outrageous Idea of Christian Scholarship* (1997), for the *Chronicle of Higher Education,* Wolfe relented a bit. Perhaps religious thought could enrich the nation's learned discourse after all. Then in October of 2000, Wolfe's article "The Opening of the Evangelical Mind" was the cover story in the *Atlantic Monthly.* In it Wolfe argued that evangelical intellectual life was substantial and vigorous, even if it is unduly constrained by evangelical colleges' insistence that their scholars pledge doctrinal fidelity. The academic world is still not fully aware of Christian scholarship, but at least Professor Wolfe has put it on the radar screen.[1]

---

1. Alan Wolfe, "The Higher Learning," *Lingua Franca* (March/April 1996): 70-77; Wolfe, "A Welcome Revival of Religion in the Academy," *The Chronicle of Higher Education*

Whether or not the academic mainstream remains interested, Christian scholarly production is showing up in the main channels of intellectual discourse. A case in point is the body of work produced by the Pew Evangelical Scholars Program. The Pew Scholars website lists four dozen titles, ranging from anthropology in the Philippines, to the philosophy of mathematics, to communication ethics, to moral psychology, to religion's role in the French Revolution, the American Civil War, and the American Civil Rights movement. The Pew Scholars publish with mainline academic and trade presses: Cambridge, Oxford, Princeton, Yale, Doubleday, Johns Hopkins, California, and Macmillan, to name a few. Skeptics might ask what makes these works Christian. Yet these books reflect assumptions, worldviews, and choices of methods and topics that are deeply influenced by their authors' Christian faith. These works are part of a broader phenomenon, for Christian scholarship is undergoing a modest renaissance just now, which is a cause for rejoicing.

A Time of Intellectual Conflict

We are deluding ourselves, however, if we assume that the road ahead for Christian scholarship will be an easy straightaway. There is a great intellectual and cultural contest going on today, what some might call a crisis of knowledge. Scientific naturalism — which for so many generations has ruled the academy and which proclaims the certainty and bias-free nature of scientific study and its promise to order and liberate all of life — is under a severe attack. Most prominent of the assailants are the postmodern anti-realists, who claim that there is no fundamental structure to be found in the universe itself. Rather, humans create all of the categories; they construe knowledge. In either case, both parties seek a way of living without reference to a divine Creator and Lawgiver — the naturalists by saying that nature is self-creating and self-regulating, and the anti-realists by saying that humanly created order is the only order there is.

According to Christian philosopher Alvin Plantinga, both parties misplace the role of humanity. Scientific naturalism reduces human be-

---

19 (September 1997): B4-5; and Wolfe, "The Opening of the Evangelical Mind," *The Atlantic Monthly* (October 2000): 55-76.

ings to the status of complicated machines, with no real creativity. The postmodern anti-realists, by contrast, substitute human beings for God by making human consciousness the source of all reality. Christian scholars may be tempted to cheer for one side or the other — for the naturalists for defending the existence of a real world that exists outside of ourselves, or for the anti-realists, who point out the failures of science to bring a consensus about how to order our lives. Christian thought, however, points to a third way. With the naturalists, it points to a real world that exists independently of our ordering of it. With the anti-realists, it has long insisted that there are no such things as purely objective facts and theories. But against both, Christian thought insists that our world only makes sense when we acknowledge the Almighty, the God of the Bible.[2]

The twin forces of scientific naturalism and postmodern anti-realism will continue to dominate our intellectual life, and Christian scholars will need to contend earnestly with them in the public arena and in university life. These debates are not merely intellectual war games. They matter out on the street. They shape the directions that societies take, the ways that people behave. How so?

For one example, both naturalism and anti-realism feed the moral relativism that plagues our civilization today. Naturalists do not believe that life can have a transcendent purpose or norms. We are driven by the blind forces of nature. Anti-realists insist that everyone structures reality differently, so it is my reckoning versus yours. They see no higher court to which one can appeal. Both points of view are abundantly present in today's worlds of business, law, politics, psychology, and popular culture. The contending parties have confused, perplexed, and paralyzed those who teach the values and patrol the boundaries of our civilization: parents, teachers, lawyers, judges, legislators, and social workers. Increasingly, it seems, we are discovering that we cannot live without moral absolutes. We see the results of moral relativism all around, and many leaders in our universities, public schools, courts of law, and businesses are saying that we need to teach values.

2. I am indebted to Alvin Plantinga for the characterizations of the two preceding paragraphs. He has laid out this argument in more detail in a number of papers and articles, but the one that I followed most closely is *The Twin Pillars of Christian Scholarship,* The Stob Lectures of Calvin College and Seminary, 1989-1990 (Grand Rapids: Calvin College and Seminary, 1990), pp. 9-28.

These two intellectual parties offer little help. "What values?" the naturalist cries. "Whose values?" responds the postmodernist. Here is an open door for Christian scholars and the Christian citizens they educate. We believe that there *is* a moral law; it is graven in large letters on the hearts of all of humanity, and societies ignore it at their peril. Christian academics have a major opportunity to contribute this wisdom to our present age. There is a hunger in our land for right relationships. People yearn for peace, good order, and human flourishing of every kind, for what the Bible calls *shalom*. We are called to seek the *shalom* of the civilization where we have been planted. May we seize the opportunity and put our scholarly talents to work, for Jesus' sake.

This, in large, simple strokes, is the challenge before us as Christian scholars. But behind it is a basic understanding of our mission that we need to grasp and hold, and by which we must be held accountable by the Christian community. And to understand this mission, we must ask some basic questions about Christian scholarship. Why are we doing this, anyway? What is our mission as Christian scholars? Why should it matter to the Christian community? How is it related to the church's mission? What do academics do to advance the church's mission? Aren't colleges optional to the church's life, especially when compared, for example, to foreign missions? What do professors have to do with the advance of the gospel, anyway?

Agents of the Great Commission

Let us look for a moment at the mission of the church, and then we can see our role in it as scholars. The Bible is rich with stories, precepts, and metaphors pointing to our chief end as children and agents of the living God. One of the most lively biblical mandates is what we call the Great Commission, Jesus' command in the Gospel of Matthew, 28:18-20:

> Then Jesus came to them and said, "All authority in heaven and on earth has been given to me. Therefore go and make disciples of all nations, baptizing them in the name of the Father and of the Son and of the Holy Spirit, and teaching them to obey everything I have commanded you. And surely I am with you always, to the very end of the age."

Christ's great commission to his church is to "go and make disciples of all nations, . . . teaching them all that I have commanded you." Typically when we read this text we see the command to proclaim personal salvation in Jesus Christ, baptize people into God's family, and teach them the Christian way. But what is this discipling of nations? It seems like an odd thought. Often, God's plan of redemption seems as though it involves only saving individuals. Yet our Savior, who claims "all authority in heaven and on earth," wants to transform a people's whole way of life. Not just individuals, but entire nations. His desire is to see the "kingdoms of this world . . . become the kingdoms of our Lord and of his Christ" (Rev. 11:15). What is God's kingdom, in which we become citizens when we profess faith in Christ and enter the fellowship of believers? The kingdom is God's full plan of redemption, the Old Testament prophets' vision of *shalom,* of that day when our world will enjoy the full reign of justice, peace, and plenty, when all of nature and society will be restored to right relationships. "Seek ye first the kingdom of God," Jesus commands us (Matt. 6:33). That is the main task of the Christian, to be a witness to and an agent for the kingdom of God. That is the work of discipleship in its fullest dimension: learning to give witness in thought, word, and deed to God's grand plan of personal, societal, global, and even cosmic redemption.

Discipleship, at its grandest scope, as in discipling the nations, is a daunting task. "If a nation is to be discipled," says Andrew Walls, the renowned missions historian, "the commanding heights of a nation's life have to be opened to the influence of Christ; for Christ has redeemed human life in its entirety. . . . Discipling a nation involves Christ's entry into the nation's thought, the patterns of relationship within that nation, the way the society hangs together, the way decisions are made."[3] There is no one cultural blueprint for how Jesus' salvation and his lordly demands will be played out in the world's incredible variety of cultures. Every generation, too, will present fresh challenges to the working out of the reign of God. The task of the gospel taking root and producing a deep and transforming expression in a culture is never over until the Lord comes to establish his kingdom fully.

Clearly, then, the church of Jesus Christ has a very broad and grand

---

3. Andrew F. Walls, *The Missionary Movement in Christian History: Studies in Transmission of Faith* (Maryknoll, N.Y.: Orbis Books, 1996), p. 51.

teaching task, and this task is central to its mission. We need to ask, however, what roles our churches are playing, as institutions, in fulfilling the Great Commission of discipling the nations. They ground people in the Scriptures and the spiritual disciplines, and introduce them to the issues pertaining to witness in the world. Compared to what someone does to prepare for his or her profession, however, the education that the average congregation provides is rather general and introductory. If Christians are to fulfill their mandate to "teach the nations," the church must go deeper and broader in this immense task. Here, I believe, is where we come in. We as Christian scholars are to be agents of cultural discipleship.

A Brief History of the Christian Academic Mission

These are not new thoughts or patterns of witness for our churches. Through the centuries, the church in the West has looked to educational institutions for help in fulfilling the Great Commission. At the turn of the last millennium, the advance of Christianity in Northern Europe was driven by the advance of learning. For missionary monks on the northern pagan frontiers, teaching the nations meant, first of all, teaching people to read and write. Northern Europe became progressively Christianized as it came under the influence of Christian education.

Eventually, groups of learning-minded graduates from the monastery schools began to form guilds to pursue learning as a community and to teach young graduates who came to them for instruction. These guilds evolved into universities, and they became a virtual third force in society, alongside church and state. Their graduates were the scholars, lawyers, pastors, and gentlemen of medieval and early modern Europe. According to historian John Van Engen, their influence on society for the sake of Christian beliefs and norms was enormous. The Reformation, you may recall, began as a disputation among university theology professors, and it produced a commitment to having well-educated pastors who could teach the Scriptures to their parishioners.[4] The mission-

---

4. John Van Engen, "Christianity and the University: The Medieval and Reformation Legacies," in *Making Higher Education Christian: The History and Mission of Evangelical Colleges in America,* ed. Joel A. Carpenter and Kenneth W. Shipps (Grand Rapids: Eerdmans, 1987), pp. 14-37.

ary task of "teaching the nations" in Northern Europe took a major leap forward during the Reformation when university scholars translated the Scriptures into the vernacular languages and developed Psalters. The gospel was taking deeper root in the culture and becoming more truly the faith of the people.

In North America, Protestant settlers quickly sought to replicate this European Christian educational mission. By 1636 the Puritan leaders of the Massachusetts Bay Colony had formed Harvard College, to educate pastors and to develop leaders for society. As American denominational missionaries sought to win the West for Christ two hundred years later, they founded colleges as strategic instruments for discipling the nation, for seeing the beliefs and values of Scripture make their way into the West's thought patterns, social structures, and modes of decision making in public affairs. The western territories rapidly became civilized, largely because of the settlers' use of Christian academies and colleges for preparing able and committed leaders.[5]

When American and European missionaries went elsewhere in the world, one of their earliest strategies was to use higher education to plant Christianity more deeply into the culture. Hence the founding of Serampore College in southeastern India in 1818 by the Baptist missionary William Carey. The college's purpose, Carey said, was the "forming of our native brethren . . . , fostering every kind of genius, and cherishing every gift and grace in them."[6] That was the beginning of a great outpouring of Protestant missionary investment in higher education. By 1935, there were more than one hundred mission-founded colleges and universities outside the North Atlantic world.[7] For the past millennium, Christians in the Western tradition have used higher education as one of their most strategic tools for fulfilling the Great Commission. We Christian scholars do not often think of ourselves as missionaries, but that is indeed our heritage. We are involved in an "intellectual apostolate," as Catholic educators put it.

This strategic partnership between church and college is not now

5. Timothy Smith, *Uncommon Schools: Christian Colleges and Social Idealism in Midwestern America, 1920-1950* (Indianapolis: Indiana Historical Society, 1978).

6. Quoted in Stephen Neill, *A History of Christian Missions* (London: Penguin Books, 1964), p. 265.

7. Dana Robert, "Shifting Southward: Global Christianity Since 1945," *International Bulletin of Missionary Research* 24 (April 2000): 51.

what it once was. We are sitting on the other side of a massive secularization of higher education. From the days of the medieval universities to the early twentieth century, Christian scholars assumed that science, philosophy, and other humane studies supported the Christian faith and advanced the gospel's mission to the nations. They also assumed that a broadly Christian approach to learning would suit the needs of the entire society. Those assumptions did not hold, for over the past century, the world of high-level inquiry and advanced education has become increasingly unwilling to support the worldview and values of Christianity.

This story is long and complex, and is masterfully related in George Marsden's *Soul of the American University*.[8] Marsden shows that two things in particular happened. The first was that the United States became more diverse culturally and religiously. As the nation became more diverse, it became more difficult for educational leaders to assume that a broad Protestant consensus could drive the purposes and content of American higher education.

The second development was in modern science. Scientific inquiry had long been considered an ally of the Christian faith, but as its influence grew as a source of knowledge and technological power, it also began to exclude other sources of knowledge. By the mid-twentieth century, scientific naturalism became the dominant view in the scholarly world. Professors with a naturalistic worldview began to argue that Christian beliefs, values, and views of the world were both intellectually outmoded and morally suspect. Beginning in earnest perhaps at the time of the Scopes Trial in the 1920s, American Protestants have encountered some major tensions between traditional Christian beliefs and views of reality on the one hand, and those driven by scientific naturalism on the other.

Mainline Protestants looked for ways to approve of the new learning and to continue to make science compatible with Christian faith. Failing that, many conceded the world of research to secular science but saved the realm of faith and values for more "spiritual" ways of knowing. This strategy carved out a niche for faith, but compared to empirical science, faith seemed less real and less relevant, and its place in intellectual life became increasingly marginal. Mainline Protestants tried to sustain a presence on university campuses with groups like the Student Christian

---

8. George M. Marsden, *The Soul of the American University: From Protestant Establishment to Established Nonbelief* (New York: Oxford University Press, 1994).

Movement and the Faculty Christian Fellowship, university chapels and chaplaincies, and divinity schools in a number of private universities. All of these efforts, however, were able to give Christian faith only a back room in the house of intellect. By the end of the 1960s, many of these efforts either ceased or had become mere shadows of their former strength.[9]

Conservative evangelical Protestants, especially of the holiness, fundamentalist, and pentecostal movements, led a general retreat from the main corridors of academic life. These groups began to favor Bible institutes, where learning the Scriptures was the focus, and without any of the more troubling forms of biblical criticism. Many of today's evangelical colleges and universities were founded as Bible schools, whose first task may have been to train evangelists and missionaries, but later began to provide spiritual inoculations for those headed to the jungles of godless higher education.[10]

These schools were fortified by a certain kind of evangelical theology that was destroying the concept of cultural discipleship. This kind of evangelical thinking narrowed God's salvation down to the personal level only, reduced the ideas of one's calling or vocation to "religious" jobs such as preaching or foreign missionary work, and devalued the Christian purpose of education except as pursued by Biblical Studies, Theology, or Practical Ministry. This change in evangelical theology is what historian Mark Noll rightly called "the intellectual disaster of fundamentalism."[11]

Through the years, however, there have been Christian colleges and Christian scholars at secular universities who have insisted that all truth is God's truth. There have been Christian professors who have argued that one's basic commitments concerning the nature and destiny of the human race and the origins and direction of the material universe shape the questions, methods, and conclusions that one brings to any field of study. There have been colleges that have insisted that all of the arts and

9. Douglas Sloan, *Faith and Knowledge: Mainline Protestantism and American Higher Education* (Louisville: Westminster/John Knox Press, 1994).

10. The best history of the Bible institute movement is Virginia Brereton, *Training God's Army: The American Bible School, 1880-1940* (Bloomington: Indiana University Press, 1990).

11. Mark A. Noll, *The Scandal of the Evangelical Mind* (Grand Rapids: Eerdmans, 1994), pp. 109-45.

sciences are relevant for preparing women and men to serve God's kingdom. These scholars and institutions may have been marginal to the greater higher education industry in America, and most of the time they have been less salient in evangelical circles than seminaries and parachurch ministries. Yet they have kept alive the idea that the kingdom of God will grow through the teaching of the nations, through the deeper conversion of cultures as well as individuals. Today, the work of these few has begun to bear fruit.[12] The idea of the integration of faith and learning has become widely accepted among the nation's evangelical colleges and universities, and I am encouraged to see how many are making this Christian intellectual task salient among their faculty and students. The "outrageous idea of Christian scholarship" is catching on with hundreds and thousands of Christian professors. It is an exciting time to be a Christian scholar.

Christian Scholarship Is Missionary Work

Given the current status of Christian scholarship, together with the ideological atmosphere of the academy, Christian scholars must recover the idea that what we are called to do as intellectuals is missionary work. We are called to bring the gospel to bear on every realm of nature and human experience. The Apostle Paul says we are to "take captive every thought to make it obedient to Christ" (2 Cor. 10:5). The mission model is crucial to what we do as Christian scholars, and this matter of cultural discipling is central to the church's mission. This we need to accept as our own calling.

We also need to impress upon the church at every turn that the Great Commission is broader than it has been commonly thought of and used in the recent past. Moreover, we need to impress upon the church that its mission of discipling nations is never finished. The assumption that the West was Christianized and that missions were to be done elsewhere, in the so-called pagan lands, deeply injured the ongoing missionary task of Western universities and their professors. Within the North Atlantic world, Christianity's influence has weakened. Our own nation is becoming increasingly crude, cruel, and pagan, and can scarcely

---

12. Noll, *The Scandal of the Evangelical Mind,* pp. 211-39 — a chapter provocatively titled "Is an Evangelical Intellectual Renaissance Underway?"

be called a Christian nation today. This can change, but it will require the partnership of church and college.

Christian scholars can make a difference, but they need to see themselves as missionaries, as kingdom agents in a lost world. They need to give witness, as intellectuals, to the kingdom in its fullness, as God's vision of *shalom*. We must keep this sense of purpose and mission clear and keen, for otherwise the secular knowledge industry will eventually assimilate and overwhelm the Christian scholars' movement of today. Yet we cannot go it alone. We need great institutional support behind our efforts, and we will find this only in a sustained and lively connection to the church, the main source of God's grace in the world today. Then, as agents of the Great Commission, Christian scholars can help the church fulfill its mandate to make disciples of all nations.

QUESTIONS FOR REFLECTION AND DISCUSSION

1. In Carpenter's judgment, scientific naturalism and postmodern anti-realism constitute the primary competitors to Christian ways of thinking. To what extent can you discern the influence of either competitor within your scholarly discipline? What scholarly questions are asked (or left unasked) and what answers are offered as a result of these influences? Are there fruitful ways in which Christian scholars can "contend earnestly" with these competing intellectual agendas?

2. What answers does Carpenter provide to the questions he raises: Why should Christian scholarship matter to the Christian community? How is it related to the church's mission? What do academics do to advance the church's mission? Aren't colleges optional to the church's life, especially when compared, for example, to foreign missions? What do professors have to do with the advance of the gospel, anyway?

3. In his brief history of Christian academic mission among American Protestants, Carpenter identifies at least three trajectories of Christian colleges during the last century, all of them responses to modernity in its various forms. These responses alternately involve degrees of accommodation, retreat, and constructive engagement. Within which trajectory does your institution best fit? What story should be told about this history? What are your own proclivities, and why?

4. Is Carpenter's affirmative response to Mark Noll's question, "Is an evangelical intellectual renaissance underway?" accurate? Why or why not?

FURTHER RELATED WORK BY THIS AUTHOR

Carpenter, Joel A., and Kenneth W. Shipps. *Making Higher Education Christian: The History and Mission of Evangelical Colleges in America.* Grand Rapids: Eerdmans, 1987.

Chapter Five

Toward a Spirituality of Higher Education

PARKER J. PALMER

There is a spiritual hunger in American higher education greater than any I have seen in the thirty years I have worked in this field. It begins with the pain felt by many academics — a pain rooted, I believe, in the shallowness of academic culture, its inability to embrace the whole of the human condition, its failure to create community, and its inadequacies in dealing with the deep problems of our time. Academics are talking about such things today in remarkably open and vulnerable ways.

Perhaps we are beginning to understand that all education is a process of spiritual formation or deformation — not just religious education, or education that has some kind of formal theological content, but *all* education. In the very act of educating we are in the process of forming or deforming the human soul. That process goes on at a level much deeper than how often a college requires students to attend chapel, how many card-carrying Christians are on the faculty, how many religion courses a student must take, or how many volumes of theology are in the library. Those markers are not irrelevant, but the spiritual formation or deformation of students — and ourselves — goes on at a much more profound level than is touched when we obsess over those kinds of externalities.

This chapter was presented as part of the H. I. Hester Lecture Series at the June 1993 meeting of the ASBCS, and adapted for this collection from the August 1993 issue of *The Southern Baptist Educator.*

75

The formation or deformation of the human soul in education begins at the very point where we create a relationship of some sort between the knower and the known. From physics to literature to psychology, we are continually modeling ways for the knower to relate to the known, which eventually become the ways an educated self relates to the world — for what world do we have, except the world as we know it? In these learning experiences we are forming or deforming a sense of self and community, whether or not we name them as spiritual formation.

This deep and abiding process goes on at the heart of what has been called the "hidden curriculum." It happens no matter what we say about our theological commitments, or about the rules and regulations that govern campus life, for it is embedded in the kind of relation we model between the educated person and the world. Across the vast sweep of American higher education, what goes on for the most part is, I am afraid, deformative because of our misguided understanding of knowledge and what it means to teach and learn. I want to suggest that we can challenge these deforming tendencies by offering an education driven by a "gospel epistemology."

The Deforming Tendencies of Objectivism

Epistemology is the philosophical study of how people know and the conditions under which their knowledge is said to be true. American colleges and universities — and the theological enterprise itself — have been deeply deformed by an epistemology, a way of knowing, that I call objectivism. Objectivism asserts that we cannot know anything truly and well until we have held ourselves at a distance from it. The educational task, then, becomes one of giving students a distant look at the facts in various fields of study in order to make sure that their knowledge is valid and pure.

Higher education is permeated with the notion that if you are not being objective, then you are not really educating. This is a very deep commitment in the academy — a commitment that comes to us from the Enlightenment, from the rise of science, and from the development of technology — and it involves distancing the knower from the world in order to gain mastery and control over it.

For example, I go around the country asking students, "When was the last time you were asked to intersect your little story with the big story under consideration in your classes?" The answer that I constantly get is, in effect, "That never happens. They teach me the big story. They want to replace my little story with the big story."

This tendency shapes not only physicists and historians and literary scholars, but also the Christian community itself, which has objectified everything from God to Jesus to Scripture to faith to ministry itself. I am talking about the objectification of Scripture so that those texts become less an engaged and engaging human journey and more a set of artifacts to be analyzed. I am talking about the way faith becomes no longer the story of our lives but a set of propositions to which we must subscribe. Thus, my concern is not just regarding the cognitive, data-driven academic disciplines, but also includes the way we have objectified the faith tradition itself.

Objectivism has three traits, as I understand it: it is a way of knowing that emphasizes objectivity, analysis, and experimentalism. Without those three words, American higher education would have little to say for itself. What do they mean?

First, objectivity suggests that we cannot know anything truly and well unless we hold ourselves at great remove from whatever we are trying to study. The great enemy in this theory of knowing is human subjectivity, which is considered utterly untrustworthy. Subjectivity is equated with darkness, error, prejudice, bias, misunderstanding, and falsehood — and is regarded with the same sympathy that Christians regard sin. I sometimes hear church folks ask, "Whatever happened to sin?" Well, the doctrine of sin is alive and well in the objectivist academy! There is an unconscious doctrine of human depravity among even the most secular educators, who are profoundly mistrustful of the subjective self and for whom knowledge can be pure and valid only if the thing known is held at arm's length and objectified, made into an object.

As soon as one makes an object out of something, the next step is to analyze it: you cut that object apart, figuratively or literally, to see what makes it tick before you have even had time to appreciate it in the round, so to speak. So the second way in which we deform souls in higher education is by inculcating them in the habit of unfettered analysis, always chopping things up, always taking things apart — with very little capacity to put things back together (just as the habit of objectivity leaves people with very little capacity to understand what is going on inside themselves).

The third thing objectivism has done is to create a mind-set called experimentalism. Once we have taken an object apart into its component parts, we move those pieces around to see whether we can create something that pleases us more than the reality that was given to us. We experiment on every level from DNA to our relation to Third World cultures. Think about experimentation for a moment, not as the act of a scientist in a laboratory, but rather as the mode in which we have related to the economically underdeveloped world. We have often said to Third World countries, "What if we took a little piece of your political system out and put some of ours in it? We think we would like you better that way." We have said, "Let us take some of your economy out and put some of ours in. We think we could deal with you more conveniently that way." We have said, "What if we took some of your religious beliefs away and replaced them with our own? We think you would be more pleasing to us that way."

Two Examples

Objectivity, analysis, and experimentalism describe the monolithic way of knowing in which we are educating students in the American academy, and they comprise a program for spiritual deformation. I can illustrate this point with two examples, one historical and one personal.

The historical example comes from a documentary film entitled *The Day After Trinity*. Trinity, of course, was the code name for the first atomic explosion at Alamogordo, New Mexico. (We Americans have a remarkable way of using religious images to label weapons of horror, as witnessed by the deadly nuclear submarine we have cruising the oceans, dubbed the *Corpus Christi* or "Body of Christ.") In this documentary, the scientists who participated in that first atomic explosion are shown as they reflect, forty-five years later, on what they had wrought. I am an aspiring pacifist, and yet I came away from that film with a real respect for the people I saw because they were so filled with reflective moral anguish.

The most remarkable moment in the documentary came when a mathematician appeared and said, in effect, "The day before we detonated that bomb, we had calculations that indicated that, when we pushed the button, there might be an instantaneous incineration of the entire envelope of oxygen surrounding the earth, thus snuffing out all forms of life on earth. The statistical chance of this happening was very, very small, but, we thought, very real." Then, he looks into the camera and says, "And yet, we pushed the button. . . ." It is an absolutely stunning moment, because when you think about it, you realize that the Trinity explosion is just one example of the experimentation that our wealth and power allow us to conduct all the time with the fate of the global society.

In this culture we say to ourselves that we are in possession of great knowledge. But the truth is that our knowledge often possesses us, in much the same way the ancients talked about demon possession. *The Day After Trinity* reveals that we are in the grip of forms of knowing that drive us to spiritually deformed lives. If we want to show concern for spiritual reformation in higher education, this is the level at which we must work. We must ask ourselves, "Are we training mathematicians, physicists, engineers, or managers who could look at an equation like that and still press the button? Are we training students in such an objective, analytic, and experimental way that we are shutting out any possibility that the Light of Christ can shine through their professional lives?"

As for my personal example of education and spiritual deformation: I was taught in some of the best institutions of higher education in this country, a couple of them church-related. I was taught by the best of scholars about a twentieth-century event called the Holocaust — an event in which six million Jews were murdered along with uncounted numbers of protesting Christians, gay men, gypsies, and anyone who did not fit the mold. But I was taught about the Holocaust in a way that left me with the sense that all of this had happened on another planet and to another species. My teachers never said, "other planet, other species." But they presented the data of that history at such antiseptic, objective distance that I was left at great remove from the realities I was learning about, and I ended up with a sense that they had nothing to do with my life.

But, of course, the Holocaust has much to do with my life, and with yours as well. I grew up in a suburb of Chicago where no Jews lived because there were systematic real estate practices in place to keep "people like them" apart from "people like us." This is a variety of the same fascism that drove the Holocaust, but I was never invited by my teachers to reflect on the connections between that big story and my little story.

Worse still, I was never asked to reflect on the fact that I have within

myself a sort of fascism of the heart: that is, a power of darkness that —
when the difference between you and me becomes too great, when your
conception of truth becomes too threatening to mine — makes me want
to kill you off. I will not do it with a gas chamber or a bullet, but with a
label, a word, a phrase, or some kind of mental dismissal that renders
you irrelevant to my life: "Oh, you're gay," or "You're a Republican," or
"You're a Baptist." I will find some way to wipe you out so that I do not
have to deal with the difference between us.

Am I arguing that my course work on the Holocaust should have
been turned into group therapy? Not at all. What I am arguing is that
when we teach people *only* in the objective, analytical, and experimental
mode, we deform their spiritual and moral lives. We create doctors who
have not the foggiest notion that there is something called mind and
spirit animating the human body. We create leaders who keep replicating
the lines drawn between enemies and the hostilities that lead to violence
on all levels. This violence is partly rooted in the violence of our knowledge — a violence perpetrated by every teacher who objectifies things
without ever letting the little story, the subjective story, the personhood
of truth enter in.

Ultimately, I am arguing not against objectivity, analysis, and experimentation, but against their hegemony. I am arguing for the richness of
holding them together with their polar opposites in a paradoxical manner. I am arguing, for example, that the objective truth of the Holocaust
should be presented in a way that opens up the subjective truths of our
students. I am arguing that the analytic skills every person needs should
be taught in a way that makes students into builders and creators, not
just people who know how to dissect the world. I am arguing that the
experimentalism on which we so heavily depend be held in creative, paradoxical tension with what I call the appreciative, the capacity to open
your hands and receive the gift of reality with respect for what you have
been given. When we approach our work with open and appreciative
hands, the quality of experimentation that emerges is quite different
from when we approach the world as raw material to be bent to our own
design.

The task for higher education is to reclaim the wholeness of what
we know about human knowledge: it is not just about distancing, it is
about intimacy as well. No scientist has ever done his or her work without having personal investment in it — and when we teach knowledge

of science, or any other field, we must find ways to invite a parallel personal investment from our students.

A Gospel Epistemology

Our special task in Christian higher education is to work toward what I call a gospel epistemology. "Gospel epistemology" is a strange combination of words — and it probably will not preach very well — but I dare to use it because we so often think of the gospel simply in terms of an ethic, or a way of living. Yet, at its deepest reaches, the gospel is a way of knowing, and if we cannot recover that way of knowing, I do not really think we can do Christian higher education or form our students in a Christian ethic.

Let me name four traits of a gospel way of knowing that have been with me in one way or another since my childhood in the Methodist Church. These are images of what it means to be a knowing person in the world that gripped my heart from the beginning of my Christian formation, images that I have not wanted to lose as I have moved through the halls of secular higher education (and through the halls of some Christian institutions that wanted to resist this way of knowing in their own special manner).

First, in the gospel way of knowing, truth is personal. That is something that my history teachers either never knew or forgot in relation to Nazi Germany. They thought truth was only propositional. They thought if I could just get the facts straight, if I could just repeat the propositions on the final exam, then I must know the truth. For them, it was all propositions all the time.

One of the most memorable things about those courses is that we never saw the photographs with corpses piled up, and we never read the poetry or saw the art produced by those who died in the camps. All we ever saw were the words of objectivist historians, and I know why: the photos, the poems, and the art were regarded as simply too subjective. They might unleash untruth among us. But for objectivists, if we can keep our study propositional and just use the abstract words, then the truth will be safeguarded.

This is not what the gospel says, however. The gospel makes the most extraordinary claim about the nature of truth that I have ever heard. When Jesus is asked, "What is truth?" the readers of John's Gospel know the answer, even though he remains silent in the face of Pilate's question. Jesus taught his disciples, "I am the way and the truth and the life" (John 14:6). He refuses to deal with the objectification of "what." He does not give us propositions — they come later with the theologians. Christ gives us personhood; he gives us himself.

As I read that claim through my own Quaker understanding, each of us is born in the form of God's image, and each of us has what Quakers have called the seed of Christ. Each of us is called to the personhood of truth, to be an incarnation of truth, and not just to recall propositions about truth. Propositions are important, but just beneath them is the personhood of whoever utters them. If you talk to any student about who his or her great teachers have been, you will not hear about the propositions they utter. Rather, you will hear about their personhood, you will hear about truth as personal. "Truth is personal" moves the educational process to a deeper level where we can engage others incarnationally and not just intellectually.

Second, in a gospel way of knowing, truth is communal. It is not enough for truth to be personal, in the diminished sense of that word — not enough for there to be "One truth for you, another truth for me, and never mind the difference." We live in this world together, and we must mind the difference. So truth in the gospel tradition is to be spoken and lived in community, and tested in a continuing communal process of dissent and consent.

Jesus not only says, "I am the Truth," but when someone asks, "How can I know the truth?" he says, "Follow me." That is, he says come into relationship; come into community. This is not the objectivist's disconnect between the big story out there and the student's little story, but an engagement of persons and subjects relating to matters of passionate concern. Truth is to emerge in dialogue and encounter, and in wrestling with relationship.

The third feature of a gospel epistemology is that truth is mutual and reciprocal. There is a very strange conceit in higher education, expressed in most college catalogs by the words, "This institution is dedicated to the pursuit of truth." According to this image, truth is out there somewhere, frantically trying to evade us — while we, with our hounds and horns, are out there chasing truth down in hopes of catching and capturing it.

But in the spiritual traditions, we know that just the reverse is the case. As Christians, we understand that we are the evasive ones, and the truth is the Hound of Heaven that continually seeks us. We are pursued by truth — and only as we come into some kind of spiritual maturity do we pursue truth as well. But the main action is in the other direction, with truth pursuing us as we try to run away from its implications. It would be a very interesting thing if academics could put down the instruments of pursuit long enough to allow truth to find us! That would lead to a very different way of teaching and learning, one we might call the gospel way.

Finally, in a gospel epistemology, truth is not only personal, communal, and reciprocal, it is also transformational. The objectivist way of knowing has persisted because it gives us the illusion that we will always be the changers and never the changed, always the transformers and never the transformed. Objectivism has persisted because it is really about power rather than knowledge — about who controls meaning, who controls institutions, and who controls the earth.

We have wanted to teach about Third World cultures in a way that allows us to look at them, but never allows them to look back at us for fear that we would have to change our lives. We have wanted to teach about the natural world in a way that allows us to look at it, but never allows it to look back at us for fear that we would have to change our lives. If you can objectify God's Word, then a few authorities can claim to control what that Word means and hold sway over others.

Objectivism — which is a complete myth with respect to how real people have ever known anything real — has great political persuasiveness because it gives us the illusion that we are in charge. But gospel truth, transformational truth, says that we are not masters but are subject to powers larger than ourselves — and that we are blessed with the chance to be co-creators of something good if we are willing to work in harmony with those larger powers.

If we embrace a gospel way of knowing, we can create a different kind of education and perhaps a different world: a world where all of us are called to embody whatever truth we know; where we gather together with others to check, correct, confirm, and deepen whatever insights we may have; where we understand that, even as we seek truth, truth is seeking us; and where there can be those vital transformations, personal and social, that might take us a step closer to the beloved community.

QUESTIONS FOR REFLECTION AND DISCUSSION

1. Palmer's central claim is, "When we teach people only in the objective, analytical, and experimental mode, we deform their spiritual and moral lives." Others might argue that in a narcissistic culture rife with therapeutic stratagems for self-fulfillment, subjectivist tendencies are more likely the culprits when it comes to moral and spiritual deformation. What sources of spiritual deformation seem most germane among your students? Given the student culture typical of your context, what kind of responsive pedagogy is most needed?
2. Is it reasonable to call the epistemological outlook embraced by Palmer a "gospel" epistemology? Does he rightly identify all of the essential attributes of a "gospel way of knowing"? With what exceptions or additions?
3. In what ways does your college or university affirm ways of personally relating to students that open up possibilities of meaningful community, mutuality, and transformation? What might be done to "take us a step closer to the beloved community" envisioned by Palmer?

FURTHER RELATED WORK BY THIS AUTHOR

Palmer, Parker J. *To Know as We Are Known: Education as a Spiritual Journey.* Rev. ed. San Francisco: HarperSanFrancisco, 1993.

————. *The Courage to Teach: Exploring the Inner Landscape of a Teacher's Life.* San Francisco: Jossey-Bass, 1998.

————. *Let Your Life Speak: Listening for the Voice of Vocation.* San Francisco: Jossey-Bass, 2000.

Part Two

Challenges and Opportunities

Chapter Six

Christian Thinking in a Time of Academic Turmoil

NATHAN O. HATCH

No issue could be more pressing at this time than the effort to address issues of Christian faith and academic life, particularly in these days of "academic turmoil." My goal is to take note of three sets of challenges that confront any of us who walk the narrow and dangerous path of higher education, who seek to be firm both in our commitment to Christian values and serious learning, and who pursue academic excellence while renewing Christian conviction. The three challenges are the following: (1) the erosion of public trust in colleges and universities, (2) the deep divorce between piety and learning that is an American heritage, and (3) the crisis of authority that grips the contemporary academic world.

My conclusion could just as well be my opening premise: that the central issue before us is that of recruiting and developing faculty who embody the kind of learning and Christian commitment on which our institutions are based. We cannot proceed with business as usual if we are to recruit faculty of learning and character, people who are not only smart and academically talented but also called to serve students, the church, and the life of the mind.

Hatch presented the Hester Lectures at the June 1992 ASBCS meeting. This chapter is adapted from the version published in the August 1992 issue of *The Southern Baptist Educator.*

NATHAN O. HATCH

The Erosion of Public Trust in Higher Education

The university in the West stands in a long tradition as a treasury of the good, the true, and the beautiful. From the medieval university to the modern liberal arts college, the academy has enjoyed privileged status as a place characterized by the search for truth, the development of moral character, and the passing on of what is prized as most worthy and noble. Institutions of higher education cling to the belief that they are set apart from self-serving and utilitarian endeavors. They aspire to serve as centers of renewal and vision for society at large. And colleges and universities generally have been accorded a kind of respect and deference not usually enjoyed by other institutions. Integrity and higher purpose are considered a natural fruit of the classroom, but not necessarily of the boardroom, courtroom, or stock exchange.

Yet increasingly, many Americans have come to question this privileged status. Indictments of higher education are leveled from many quarters. Spiraling costs and renewed concern about the quality of undergraduate teaching have led to intense scrutiny of faculty and university administrators alike. Confidence in universities has also been diminished by the nation's lack of international competitiveness in technical fields, by celebrated cases of scientific fraud, by new racial strife on campus, and by athletic abuses. Professional schools in law, medicine, and business are criticized for cranking out graduates who demonstrate commitment to little else than financial gain. And in recent days politicians and the media have used controversies over indirect costs and "political correctness" to tar universities with the brush of greed and intolerance. This rising tide of criticism, wave upon wave, has eroded the esteem once accorded the academy. "Not that long ago, it was generally assumed that higher education was an investment in the future of the nation," Ernest L. Boyer observes. But there "is a growing feeling in this country that higher education is, in fact, part of the problem rather than the solution — going still further, that it's become a private benefit, not a public good."[1]

The problem is compounded by divisions within the university itself over issues such as the curriculum and the roles of research and teaching.

---

1. Ernest L. Boyer, "The Scholarship of Engagement," in *Selected Speeches 1979-1995* (Princeton: Carnegie Foundation for the Advancement of Teaching, 1997), p. 85.

Disciplines are increasingly more specialized, less capable of communicating with each other and with a literate lay audience about the broader purposes of education. Debates about deconstruction and revising the literary canon also have been broadcast far beyond the walls of the academy, resulting in competing visions about the ultimate goals of a liberal arts education. A decade ago the humanities made a plausible argument that professional education should incorporate more of the humanities; today, the crisis of confidence within their own disciplines puts the humanities in a poor position to offer advice. Fierce public controversy over National Endowment for the Arts (NEA) funding has also chipped away at the broad public support once enjoyed by academics in the fine arts. And the NEA seems increasingly embroiled in debates over political ideology.

Even church-related institutions, both Catholic and Protestant, have engaged in considerable soul searching in recent years about their distinctive missions. What kind of role should they assume in the diverse tapestry of American higher education? Since the 1960s, many of these institutions have moved dramatically into the mainstream of American higher education, losing much of their religious or ethnic particularity. This change of identity now raises questions about what kind of community these institutions should serve and what kinds of traditions and values they should embody. Whatever direction our institutions choose to take amidst these issues, we, as never before, will have to articulate and defend our essential mission.

My point here is a simple one: that none of us in higher education can afford to place our institutions on autopilot, allowing conventional wisdom and traditional practice to govern our approach. To restore confidence in our institutions, we must carefully think through our institutional purposes and strategies and set deliberate courses of action. This will not be easy or simple, given the multiple and conflicting pressures and constituencies that our schools represent.

But this period of ferment and questioning does offer great opportunity. This is a time for fresh vision, new alliances, and energetic leadership. As society at large grows increasingly frustrated with the uncertain trumpet sounding from modern higher education, Christian institutions have an unusual opportunity to articulate what may be the only coherent educational philosophy in the marketplace. The storm over the university at large offers Christian institutions a clear opportunity to assert their distinctives.

The Divorce between Piety and Learning

Academics committed to the vitality of the church have come up against a rude stumbling block in the record of the last century-and-a-half. In the Western democracies, at least, there is strong evidence that the vitality of churches, Catholic or Protestant, has run inversely proportional to the influence of intellectuals in church life. In Europe and in Great Britain, where succeeding generations of university theologians have kept the church abreast of contemporary intellectual ferment, the overall influence of the church has declined precipitously, leaving a coterie of erudite theologians talking largely to themselves. In the United States, by contrast, Protestant and Catholic churches have never taken intellectual moorings that seriously. They have tacked to far more popular winds. As a result, churches are still remarkably filled on Sunday mornings — still over 40 percent of the population — even as intellectuals bemoan the lack of respect for Christian thinking within and without the churches. Such evidence led William F. Buckley to exclaim that he would sooner be governed by a church whose bishops were chosen by the first five hundred names from the Chicago phone directory than by a bunch of bishops made up of university professors.

My point is that in twentieth-century America, most empirical evidence suggests that custodians of the mind — colleges and universities — do more to undermine rather than support religious life. What is discouraging is not just the pervasive secularization of higher education in the twentieth century, but also the feeble efforts of church-related institutions to retain a distinctive Christian character.

Yet secularization is only one of the dangers most of us face. Threatening our institutions from the other flank are forms of religious populism that make it difficult to carry out serious intellectual life. This state of affairs is utterly consistent with patterns in the history of American Christianity: the driving force of American Christianity for over 150 years has been its popular or democratic orientation, and those forms of Christianity that have prospered are those that can rally popular support.

Consequently, in contemporary America we find the paradoxical situation of increasing religious commitment in one sector of society accompanied by more entrenched secularism in another. Religion is abounding in the realms of popular culture, among less-educated people, and in ways that concentrate on breadth of audience rather than

90

depth of insight. In the realms of high culture — in the best universities, in the arts, in literary circles — the juggernaut of secularism rolls on, pressing religious belief into territory that is smaller and of less consequence.

The problem is the vast expanse between the secularism of elite culture, on the one hand, and the burgeoning world of popular Christianity on the other. The English sociologist David Martin comments that while both England and America share an anti-intellectual populism, in America such populists have worked within rather than without the walls of the church.[2] Populist forms of Christianity depict reality in layman's terms. They are not anti-intellectual *per se* but want to depict reality in ways capable of being grasped by a broad range of people. This approach reminds one of what Dr. Johnson said about learning in Scotland: "that it is like bread in a besieged town, where everyone gets a little but no man a full meal." This often means that uncomfortable complexity is flattened out, that issues are resolved by a simple choice of alternatives, and that fine distinctions are lost in the din of ideological battle. In these camps there is little fear that further reduction of content for popular consumption could at times involve downright falsification.

This populist approach to intellectual matters is evident in the defense of creationism, of the inerrancy of the Bible, and of the refutation of "secular humanism." All three of these issues are much more likely to be treated in ways that rally a large constituency than in ways that admit of the genuine complexity of the issues and that allow scholars to retreat from pitched battle to carefully weigh and clarify the issues at hand. The problem is that those who most vigorously protest the danger of "secular humanism," for instance, are often least capable of winning the right to be heard by contemporary intellectuals.

Populist engagement in theological debate has three crippling effects upon the ongoing task of Christian thinking. First, it reinforces the view of secular academics that Christians have nothing to say that is intellectually coherent and compelling. Second, it defines issues in ways that make it difficult for Christian scholars to undertake creative and foundational scholarship. To transgress the categories as they have come to be popularly defined is to become suspect. Considerable energy is spent in

2. David Martin, *A General Theory of Secularization* (New York: Harper and Row, 1978), pp. 50, 90.

intramural wrangling rather than attempting to address issues that are fundamental to the Christian faith. In this sense, it is the people who are the custodians of orthodoxy, and their leaders will rally them to the cause of ferreting out those scholars who are not theologically safe. A third difficulty is that populist forces within the church sometimes accelerate the forces of secularization within our own institutions. How easy it is, when avoiding fundamentalist control on the one hand, to slip into an open-mindedness that in the name of academic freedom evaporates anything distinctly Christian. For example, an unintended result of fundamentalist resurgence among Southern Baptists may be to send many educators and institutions in the same direction taken by Duke, Emory, and Southern Methodist — schools that superbly serve the broader society but retain few distinctively Christian elements outside of their divinity schools.

I am suggesting a different path that avoids slipping into secularism on the one hand and giving up serious thought and scholarship on the other — higher education that is unflinching in its commitment both to Christian values and to serious learning. The American experience has few models of colleges that have retained Christian conviction while pursuing academic excellence. The traditions in American higher education are much more bifurcated, with vital forms of Christianity proceeding with little intellectual muscle and with those Christians attuned to the life of the mind readily succumbing to the secularizing dictates of modern education. Nonetheless, the challenge of Christian thinking calls us to struggle to hold together elements that American culture has often defined as incompatible, and to steer a middle course between what are often stark and incorrectly defined alternatives. Vital faith and deep learning are neither like oil and water, incapable of mixing, nor like twin components of a zero-sum game, the quantity of one increasing at the expense of the other. A Christian college or university has no higher calling than that of preserving the marriage of faith and learning.

The Crisis of Authority in the Modern University

Unfortunately, the task of holding faith and learning together is made doubly hard by the crisis of authority that plagues the modern world of serious scholarship. Christian scholars will find few stable points of reference either in the disciplines they are studying or in the theological frames of reference that are currently available. Thus, the intellectual environment in which we now live is itself a major stumbling block to the union of faith and scholarship. The character of present-day scholarship makes it difficult for scholars seeking to work from a Christian starting place to come to grips with their disciplines in constructive ways. Where does one find a solid position from which to assess the fluid instability all around?

There are at least two reasons why difficulty exists for Christians to locate trustworthy maps or compasses in the contemporary world. One might think of these as two concentric circles: the first and broadest dimension of the problem concerns the underlying crisis of authority in the contemporary academic world. We can picture the second ring of the circle as the theological instability that besets the Christian church.

The modern intellectual world is adrift, incapable or unwilling to allow any claim of certainty to set the coordinates by which others are to be judged. The dominant forces work toward fragmentation, the limitations of reason, and a breakdown of dogmatic verities — what Charles Krauthammer has called the Balkanization of American education. Examples can readily be found in virtually every scholarly discipline and every area of intellectual life, but a few should suffice to illustrate my point:

Literary Criticism   No discipline reveals the current state of intellectual disjointedness so clearly as literary criticism. Deconstructionism undermines the idea that literary texts have any objective meanings intended by their authors or inherent in the text. Instead, deconstructionists either embrace the fragmentation of a work resulting from its "deconstruction," or they relocate meaning in the understanding of the reader. The upshot of this line of thinking is revealed in a book by Barbara Herrnstein Smith, the former president of the Modern Language Association. *Contingencies of Value* champions what can only be called a hardcore relativism, in which the meaning of any work of literature is to be found only in the understanding of the individual reader. Smith goes even further to argue that every reader's interpretation is just as good as another's. By the end of the book Smith has taken her reasoning to its logical conclusion, suggesting that radical relativism is the only appropriate standard for moral questions as well as aesthetic questions. Her final conclusion: "There is no *bottom* bottom line anywhere."[3]

History   Historical studies went through its first crisis of authority in the 1930s when a group of influential American historians began to poke holes in the pretensions of those who aspired after total historical objectivity. The subsequent intellectual crisis occasioned by the rise of totalitarianism sent academicians scurrying away from their relativist arguments, but the social upheaval of the 1960s stimulated a new wave of radical relativism among historians. Since that time the historical profession has become, in the words of C. Vann Woodward, "fragmented beyond hope of unification."[4] The standards that previously guided historians have faded from view with each person guided primarily by "that which [is] right in [one's] own eyes."[5] As a result, confusion, not clarity, prevails throughout the discipline.

Law   Legal studies also face increasing confusion as a result of an onslaught of relativism. The attack has come on two fronts, the practical and the theoretical. On the practical side, legal scholars have expressed increasing dismay with the lack of continuity in judicial decisions, especially those dealing with constitutional law. The American legal system has always been based on the premise that similar cases will be judged similarly, and that there ought to be continuity and predictability in the law. But Supreme Court decisions in the last fifteen years have defied rational categorization, resulting in an increasing tendency to what can only be termed situational jurisprudence. On the theoretical side, a school of thought calling itself Critical Legal Scholarship has challenged the assumption that law is based on the attempt to approach an absolute standard of justice. This school argues instead that law is merely an extension of politics, constantly changing as the goals of those who make and enforce the law change. The result of both these shifts in direction has been to leave legal scholars groping in confusion as the profession lurches toward thoroughgoing relativism.

3. Barbara Herrnstein Smith, *Contingencies of Value: Alternative Perspectives for Critical Theory* (Cambridge, Mass.: Harvard University Press, 1988), p. 149.

4. C. Vann Woodward, "Truth and Consequences," *The New Republic* (20 February 1989): 42.

5. Woodward, "Truth and Consequences," p. 43.

Undergraduate Curriculum   Loud and public debates over university and high school curricula have become commonplace. Allan Bloom, Lynne Cheney, and Martha Nussbaum follow a long line of public intellectuals who argue that the failure of students to know the great works of Western civilization has left them impoverished.[6] At the same time, at Stanford and many other places, faculty wish to replace Western-oriented, male-dominated education with that which represents women, minorities, and people of color. In *The Disuniting of America,* Arthur M. Schlesinger, Jr. worries that we are losing any common national identity as rival ethnic groups retell the American experience from their own point of view. "Will the melting pot yield to the Tower of Babel?" he asks.[7]

The positive side of this ferment in academia is that toleration has become a principal virtue of our age, meaning that marginal groups (even Christians) are accorded far more respect than they were earlier in the twentieth century. The danger, of course, is that the gentle lamb of toleration often returns as the wolf of relativism. This has produced the turmoil and confusion that prevails in so many of the academic disciplines today. Christians are both better off and worse off — better, in the sense of being tolerated like everyone else; worse, because claims to truth no longer carry weight.

The problem is compounded by the rapid disintegration of church authorities in recent years. The Roman Catholic Church provides the most vivid example. Since Vatican II, the largest Christian church in the world has set out to update its witness to the gospel. In the process it has overturned patterns of language and liturgy going back fifteen hundred years, of church polity going back a thousand years, and of theology going back over five hundred years. The subsequent turmoil is something to behold — heartening in its return to Scripture and lay involvement,

6. See Allan Bloom, *The Closing of the American Mind* (New York: Simon and Schuster, 1987); Lynne V. Cheney, *American Memory: A Report on the Humanities in the Nation's Public Schools* (Washington, D.C.: National Endowment for the Humanities, 1987), *Humanities in America* (Washington, D.C.: National Endowment for the Humanities, 1988), and *50 Hours: A Core Curriculum for College Students* (Washington, D.C.: National Endowment for the Humanities, 1989); and Martha Nussbaum, *Cultivating Humanity: A Classical Defense of Reform in Liberal Education* (Cambridge, Mass.: Harvard University Press, 1997).

7. Arthur M. Schlesinger, *The Disuniting of America* (New York: W. W. Norton, 1992), p. 18.

heart-rending in its confusion and bitter recriminations among the parties. Shattered is the Thomistic intellectual synthesis that had been the dominant and unifying force in Catholic intellectual life. In its place, one finds claimants to intellectual authority that are as diverse as the spectrum between Protestant fundamentalists and liberals. A century ago, Protestants such as John Henry Newman who were troubled by a crisis of authority could find a safe haven in the Church of Rome. Today, the full force of the tempest has reached even those shores, leaving thoughtful Catholics few stable intellectual moorings amidst a bewildering range of theological options.

The Catholic experience is symptomatic of a much broader trend of powerful and synthetic theologies everywhere on the wane. Protestant, Calvinist, Lutheran, and Baptist orthodoxies are showing themselves to be less and less capable of sustaining internal cohesion and a vital intellectual life. As sociologist Robert Wuthnow points out in *The Restructuring of American Religion,* since World War II, even civil religion, which is so often employed to legitimize the national purpose, has been fractured into two loudly discordant camps.[8]

Whatever distinctives there are in Baptist, Catholic, Lutheran, or Reformed identity, they are hardly self-evident in the current climate. Christian scholars will find few stable points of reference either in disciplines they are studying or in theological frames of reference that are currently available. Graduate students and young scholars will need encouragement, time, and support to find stable moorings in these heavy seas. Do not underestimate the difficulty of their task.

The Vital Role of Christian Faculty

What then do I make of all this sober musing — the erosion of public confidence in higher education, and the divorce of faith from learning at the same time the academy seems intellectually adrift and rudderless? All I have said comes down to a simple point: How do we recruit and cultivate the faculty whom we will expect collectively to embody the ideals of our institutions?

8. Robert Wuthnow, *The Restructuring of American Religion: Society and Faith Since WWII* (Princeton: Princeton University Press, 1988).

College faculty and administrators have no greater responsibility than to nurture a new generation of Christian thinkers. This means going the second mile to shepherd the young people who have the potential to be the next generation of Christian scholars. In an age when fewer of our very best students are willing to make the sacrifices required of an academic career, we must lead them to take up the calling of teaching and scholarship. In an age of bewildering intellectual confusion, we must assist Christians in graduate school to keep their moorings, to form relationships with other Christian students and professors in their disciplines. In an age of endless burdens upon administrators, presidents and deans must spend a tremendous amount of time and energy looking for the best faculty, models of mature Christian reflection. We must leave no stone unturned. And after scholars have come to call our institutions their academic home, we must do everything in our power to revitalize their efforts in teaching and research.

Attracting and developing faculty is our single most important job, the one responsibility that should elicit our greatest creativity. To make a tenured appointment or a tenure-track appointment is to confront a multi-million dollar investment. More importantly, each appointment in a college or university becomes a finite embodiment of what that institution will be for the next generation. It is an effort that should never become routine and one for which we should gladly go the second mile.

This is true in any institution, but much more so at a Christian college or university. In addition to seeking excellence in teaching and research, we also want to find people of faith, character, integrity, and commitment — people who undertake their responsibilities as a vocation. This is a difficult assignment indeed. Let me be somewhat practical. How then do we attract and develop faculty in ways that are not routine? I would like to suggest three strategies for attracting faculty.

The first strategy has to do with creative leadership at the department level. Few academic departments improve themselves by a democratic process alone. There is tremendous inertia in departments. Furthermore, in contemporary academic life, there is tremendous force toward the periphery, toward pluralism, and toward different points of view — a tremendous centrifugal force. Sometimes it is methodological pluralism. At other times, extremely diverse points of view about religion divide faculty in a department or division. In these and many other ways, interests are pulling away from the center. The result is that search committees are somewhat dicey. In this mix, there can be nothing more important than department chairs that the university can trust to embody the mission of the university. Without that critical gatekeeper, it is very difficult to build excellent departments, to build departments that in any sense can be called Christian. The first strategy, then, is to make sure that those who lead departments embody the finest ideals of the university.

The second strategy involves professional engagement. In some ways, I think the worst way in the world to make an appointment is merely to announce an opening, interview at a convention, bring three to five people to campus, and make a hire. If that is all we do, we are in deep trouble. Departments have to be deeply professionally engaged. They have to know where other good departments are and the kinds of methodologies that are being used. They have to be known as good departments, so that good scholars recommend their best graduate students to them. Furthermore, we must be professionally engaged so that we know who in the discipline are young teachers of Christian commitment. We have to be more creative about knowing the available talent and in making appointments beyond the entry level. It is very difficult at professional conventions and during brief on-campus interviews to explore meaningfully the questions of Christian identity and to see whether someone is an appropriate fit. How much better it is to know what someone's character is, to have some kind of track record, and on that basis to recruit them to campus.

The third issue is that of responsiveness or flexibility. Too often appointments are locked in by departmental assignment and budgeting restraints. Departments narrow the field even more in their need to cover sub-disciplines. We have to be responsive to look for the best people and move quickly if they become available. If issues of character and belief and of faith and learning are important, it may well mean that disciplinary specialization may have to be compromised and that budgets may have to be stretched in a given year to accomplish a "target of opportunity" appointment.

In being flexible, I would also encourage us to look beyond mere denominational labels. Building a faculty of Christian scholars in this day and age will require looking for people of orthodox belief beyond any one denomination. In short, I think it is difficult for any religiously affiliated institution, whether Baptist, Lutheran, Church of Christ, or Catholic, to build a quality faculty exclusively from within their own walls. Notre Dame finds some of its best allies in the cause of building a Christian university to be people like Alvin Plantinga and George Marsden. At the same time, it is often nominal Catholics who are most anxious that Notre Dame shed its religious distinctives.

Ernest Boyer has said that there is no such thing as institutional renewal. There is only people renewal. In the same vein, let me underscore the point that our institutional aspirations have few ways of being realized other than by the people who constitute our faculty. Christian thinking will be sustained in the modern world only as we do what it takes to recruit and nurture those young persons who have the ability and the calling to serve as Christian intellectuals.

QUESTIONS FOR REFLECTION AND DISCUSSION

1. On Hatch's account, the erosion of public trust in higher education provides both a challenge and an opportunity for Christian colleges and universities. To what extent has Christian higher education been tainted in the public eye by the same tendencies eroding trust in higher education more generally? Is the extension of these public worries to Christian higher education warranted? Hatch suggests, "The storm over the university at large offers Christian institutions a clear opportunity to assert their distinctives." How would the Christian academy's response to faltering public confidence in higher education be different from the responses of the academy at large?

2. Can Christian colleges and universities bridge the "vast expanse between the secularism of elite culture . . . and the burgeoning world of popular Christianity"? Hatch suggests an affirmative response, but notes that "the American experience has few models of colleges that have retained Christian conviction while pursuing academic excellence," suggesting previous failures in such efforts. What risks from church and culture do attempts to bridge the gap pose? What risks are posed by not addressing this problem?

3. Hatch describes a crisis of authority that touches not only the modern university, but also the church, leaving Christian scholars with few stable moorings. How has this challenge shaped your experience, either individually or institutionally? To what theological and disciplinary touchstones would you turn, and why? What kinds of institutional responses to this difficulty are appropriate?

4. Assuming that Christian faculty play the vital role Hatch maintains, what more should you do personally, departmentally, and institutionally to build a faculty of Christian scholars, both for the present and the future?

FURTHER RELATED WORK BY THIS AUTHOR

Hatch, Nathan O. *The Democratization of American Christianity.* New Haven: Yale University Press, 1989.

Noll, Mark A., George M. Marsden, and Nathan O. Hatch. *The Search for Christian America.* Rev. ed. Colorado Springs: Helmers & Howard, 1989.

Chapter Seven

The Closing of the American Mind and the Opening of the Christian Mind: Liberal Learning, Great Texts, and the Christian College

ARTHUR F. HOLMES

In his famous indictment of contemporary university education, Allan Bloom claims that we have witnessed "a change in our view of things moral and political as great as the one that took place when Christianity replaced Greek and Roman paganism."[1] We might be tempted to dismiss this as rhetoric, an exaggeration for the sake of effect, or just one more acknowledgment of the secularization of the West that began in the Enlightenment and has gradually been producing a post-Christian culture. But Bloom develops his thesis by talking about the values of today's students, so that we are compelled to ask ourselves how far the symptoms he describes are evident on the Christian campus, and how the mission of the Christian college relates to this invasion of post-Christian values.

I therefore want to examine the perennially troubling symptoms Bloom describes, along with his diagnosis and his prescription for reversing the tide. Then I want to say something about the mission of the Chris-

1. Allan Bloom, *The Closing of the American Mind* (New York: Simon and Schuster, 1987), p. 141.

Holmes presented the Hester Lectures at the 1988 meeting of the ASBCS, and adapted this chapter from versions of the lectures published in the September 1988 issue of *The Southern Baptist Educator.*

tian college, and particularly about the integration of faith and learning, in these regards. In so doing, I will argue that while much of Bloom's description accurately identifies troubling tendencies of the young adults who today pursue university education, his response — a liberal education grounded in the "great texts" — is of itself insufficient to set things right. Rather, I maintain that a liberal education grounded in Christian commitment is the best, surest solution to minds otherwise closed to the truth.

The Closing of the American Mind

Bloom's Three Symptoms

Bloom identifies three symptoms worthy of concern for those committed to the traditional aims of liberal education. First is value relativism. Students assume as if it were self-evident, he points out, that truth is relative: the current talk is of differences in "lifestyle," of "sexual preference," of openness to all points of view — uncritically, as if no objective considerations have any bearing, as if truth and falsity, right and wrong, do not even exist. If everything is relative, moreover, then we can learn nothing from history, for yesterday's truth may not apply today, and no common good for all can be uncovered. Values are reduced to subjective feelings, and preferences are rooted, if anywhere at all, in an individual's distinctive psychological or biological makeup or a society's need for survival.

This is a familiar picture, one to which C. S. Lewis alerted us years ago in *The Abolition of Man,* with its account of a writing textbook that admitted only two kinds of language: factual description and emotive expression. So on this view when the poet talks of a sublime waterfall, said Lewis, he in effect talks not of the waterfall but of the feelings he has at beholding the waterfall; not sublime feelings, however, but the very opposite — feelings of insignificance and awe.[2] Value relativism boils down to a sheer subjectivism in which we impose our own feelings on things that objectively, in themselves, have no value at all.

Hence, Bloom's second symptom is the loss of any worldview that can ground values in reality. No moral universe such as we find in Plato, or for that matter in the Old Testament prophets, is even envisioned. In

2. C. S. Lewis, *The Abolition of Man* (New York: Macmillan, 1947), pp. 13ff.

a world of bare fact without intrinsic value, we are given a kind of political liberalism devoid of the universal natural rights that first vouchsafed to all the liberty to be liberals at all. What we call rights are simply our wants and desires, but wants and desires afford no logical grounds for natural rights. So what? They can be won by rhetoric or force.

Meanwhile, says Bloom, this lack of any basis in reality for values has robbed us of any sense of the breadth and depth of evil; for without an objective basis evil, like good, becomes purely subjective and relative, something we simply happen to dislike or find painful. I am reminded of my graduate school advisor, a repentant relativist, who was shocked out of his relativism when, faced with the stark reality of the Holocaust, he found himself crying, "That's wrong!" He came to call himself a "theist-at-large": "at-large" because he remained uncommitted to any particular faith, but a "theist" because objective right and wrong must have an unchanging basis in a reality that is itself moral being.

In the 1950s Elizabeth Anscombe, the British Catholic philosopher, published an article entitled "Modern Moral Philosophy," in which she decried the absence of moral duty and moral law in the previous half-century of utilitarian ethics.[3] Yet, she asked, how can there be moral law without a moral lawgiver? Today's value relativism stems from the loss of belief in a moral universe, from the rejection of that theistic worldview which since ancient times has undergirded the values of both the church and Western culture. The assumption that this is a value-free universe shows up plainly in student goals. A recent UCLA survey found that "to be very well off financially" was one of the top personal goals ranked in 1999 by 70.4 percent of freshmen, up from 39.1 percent in 1970, while developing a "meaningful philosophy of life" dropped from 82.9 percent in 1967 to 41.1 percent in 1999.[4] The view of life this implies is best described as uncritical egoism.

Bloom's third symptom takes us still further, to a lack of personal identity, the absence of any ideal for adult maturity. Preoccupation with "finding myself" and with "self-realization," after all, are just extensions of the age-old question, "Who am I?" This sense of inner emptiness, this

3. Elizabeth Anscombe, "Modern Moral Philosophy," *Philosophy* 33 (1958): 1-19.
4. See Linda J. Sax et al., *Designing an Assessment of the First College Year: Results from the 1999-2000 YFCY Pilot Study* (Los Angeles: UCLA Higher Education Research Institute, 2000), p. 44.

personal vacuity, comes from the starkness of an outer world emptied of intrinsic meaning and purpose. How in such a world does one gain any sense of personal value, any meaning-giving identity? What does it matter who I am or who I become? How do I decide my personal goals, or educational goals for that matter? Logically, I am reduced to what Jean-Paul Sartre described as "a bubble of consciousness in an ocean of nothingness" — until the bubble pops.

Now to what extent are these three symptoms (value relativism, the loss of a worldview to ground our values, and the lack of personal identity) apparent in the Christian college? How could they be absent in a shrunk world whose values are disseminated by pop music, by mass media, and by the entertainment and advertising industries? Our students are certainly not insulated from these forces, nor can they be.

Undoubtedly a Christian upbringing makes some difference: William Perry's "dualist" stage in moral development is likely to be both more pronounced and more prolonged. And undoubtedly many of our students have learned a language about the will and purpose of God that seems to belie the charge of relativism, loss of worldview, or lack of personal identity. Yet it remains a question whether individually they have moved beyond conditioned, clichéd responses, to an interiorized life commitment with basic beliefs and values clearly understood and firmly held. We just do not have good data on Christian college students vis-à-vis Perry's three stages — dualism, relativism, and commitment.[5] But in any case, the ethos of the day invades our minds and campuses, making the task of Christian higher education not only more needful but more difficult as well.

Bloom's Diagnosis

But let us turn from the symptoms to Bloom's diagnosis, his explanation of what has brought about the situation we have been describing. He attributes today's value relativism to the influence of Nietzsche, whose notion of "Beyond Good and Evil" overtly embraced subjectivism, and of Max Weber, who taught us to use the vague term "values" in this de-

---

5. See William G. Perry, *Forms of Intellectual and Ethical Development in the College Years* (New York: Holt, Rinehart and Winston, 1970), for an account of these common stages of moral and intellectual development.

scriptive and relativist sense for the subjective "posits" we make. But as far as the British and American scene is concerned, I am convinced that he grossly underestimates the influence of the scientific mentality represented by modern empiricism and positivism, for it is there that fact and value fell apart and the post-Christian view emerged of a world devoid of all intrinsic value.[6] Value relativism arose as part of the so-called scientific worldview.

Let me elaborate a little on this historical story. That the Judeo-Christian worldview accords inherent purpose and worth to all creation, and in particular to human persons, is quite plain. The biblical refrain, "it is good," repeated time and again in the Genesis creation story, represents God's moral judgment about everything he had made. Creation has moral worth to God himself, not just in relation to the individual self-interest and feelings of human beings. This worth of the creation undergirds the history of redemption: it is premised by the gospel itself, that God so loved this world. It undergirds the creation mandate to cultivate the earth and educate its inhabitants. It grounds both the scientific and the artistic enterprises in their quest for understanding and for beauty. And it provides not only an environmental ethic but also an appeal to natural moral law.

The Greco-Roman tradition was somewhat analogous, as the early church fathers recognized. Being, Plato declared, is good, and this world of change can only exist by participating in the good. For his student, Aristotle, this meant that everything has its natural good, an essential *telos* built into the very nature of things. And the Stoics in their turn found in nature a *logos* structure that gave the world an order that is good.

Western culture arose from the confluence of these two streams, the Judeo-Christian and the Greco-Roman. Their compatibility in rooting values in nature made possible the medieval synthesis, not only in theology and philosophy, but in science, art, ethics, and politics as well. Indeed, this synthesis constituted an entire worldview.

The crucial change began when the scientific revolution of the seventeenth and eighteenth centuries replaced Aristotle's teleology with inert matter and blind mechanical forces. Matter has spatial qualities like size, shape, and density, but color, taste, and smell are "secondary" quali-

6. This separation of fact from value is the story traced in Arthur F. Holmes, *Fact, Value, and God* (Grand Rapids: Eerdmans, 1997).

ties, existing only in an observer's subjective experience. Aesthetic values now had no objective basis. As Alfred North Whitehead puts it:

> Thus nature gets credit which should in truth be reserved for ourselves: the rose for its scent, the nightingale for its song, and the sun for its radiance. . . . [But] Nature is a dull affair, soundless, scentless, colorless; merely the hurrying of material, endlessly, meaninglessly.[7]

It is of this world that Tennyson wrote in his *In Memoriam:*

> 'The stars,' she whispers, 'blindly run;
> A web is woven across the sky;
> From out waste places comes a cry,
> And murmurs from the dying sun:
>
> 'And all the Phantom, Nature, stands —
> With all the music in her tone,
> A hollow echo of my own, —
> A hollow form with empty hands.'
>
> And shall I take a thing so blind,
> Embrace her as my natural good;
> Or crush her, like a vice of blood,
> Upon the threshold of the mind?[8]

— which is what Enlightenment rationalism and its scientific mentality sought to do, namely to squeeze all the knowledge possible out of nature. Tennyson's "waste places" and that "hollow echo" reverberate in T. S. Eliot's "The Hollow Men":

> We are the hollow men
> We are the stuffed men
> Leaning together
> Headpiece filled with straw. . . .[9]

7. Alfred North Whitehead, *Science and the Modern World* (New York: Macmillan, 1929), p. 80.

8. Alfred, Lord Tennyson, *In Memoriam,* ed. Vernon P. Squires (New York: Silver, Burdett, and Co., 1906), p. 34.

9. T. S. Eliot, *The Complete Poems and Plays* (New York: Harcourt, Brace and Co., 1934), p. 56.

— with no intrinsic worth, in a worldview that separates values from reality.

What I am indicting in this scientific mentality is a twofold thing. On the one hand it regards nature as value-free facts to be explained and exploited without reference to either intrinsic or transcendent purpose. On the other hand, it regards human knowledge as purely objective, detached, and value-free. We see the beginnings of it in people like John Locke who derived all knowledge from simple empirical data.

But the unity-of-science movement more fully epitomized the thing in its insistence that all knowledge meet scientific criteria, and only scientific knowledge counts. Auguste Comte initiated this in the nineteenth century by extending empirical methods to the study of social structures and processes, and to ethics. Bentham and Mill simply picked up on it in proposing a utilitarianism that makes ethics a matter of cost-benefit management in the pursuit of what we desire. This scientific exclusivism came to its climax in the twentieth-century logical positivist claim that, if empirical data are indispensable, the moral oughts and obligations of normative ethics reduce to emotive expressions of subjective feeling, and any theological or metaphysical assertions become factually empty gobbledygook. "Headpiece filled with straw," indeed.

This is how the notions of presuppositionless science, value-free science, and value-free education arose: the separation of nature from value led to eliminating values from the cognitive domain. Value-free education proved to be an empty dream, an illusory will-o'-the-wisp. But without an underlying worldview to reunite reality to value, values are still all at sea, free-floating subjective feelings, and all we have to replace value-free science and education is value relativism. And value-relative education is precisely what Bloom indicts. He blames Nietzsche and Weber, but skips over the impasse that drove us there, the impasse created by this scientific mentality.[10] In assimilating the epistemology of modern science, our universities were seduced into scientific exclusivism. The closing of the American mind is at its root the closing of the scientific mind to anything but scientific-type knowledge and scientific method.

This revised diagnosis explains two of Bloom's symptoms: value rel-

---

10. I think the connection between Nietzsche and the scientific mentality is problematic since he rejects the certainty of science as well as that of religion.

ativism and the loss of a worldview that grounds values in reality. But what about Bloom's third symptom, the lack of personal identity? Here too what I have called "the scientific mentality" plays a major part: empirical objectivity excludes those factors that give distinctively human identity and individual worth. Bloom points in passing to the account given by that father of empiricism, John Locke. Locke ascribes the sense of personal identity simply to memory, with its continuity of an individual's consciousness, intermittent though it is, from the past into the present.

What else could empiricism come up with? "I know myself," Locke thinks, "just as an ephemeral collection of sensations and inner awarenesses — an unsure foundation for the natural rights." Locke wants to ascribe this to us all. Little wonder, Bloom concludes, that Nietzsche more strongly appeals to the modern mind, for with no other basis than empiricism available, we must create not only our own values, but our own personal identity as well. When scientific exclusivism failed to give personal identity, then Nietzsche and Weber caught us on the rebound.

We plainly need a far fuller account of what constitutes a person than empiricism or science alone can give. Christian writers in psychology have pointed out the way.[11] What more is there to personal identity than Locke and his descendants have given us? We might want to say, "a soul, of course!" But Locke himself believed we have both soul and body — he simply followed Descartes in that regard, and that was his problem. For just as Descartes argued from "I think" (meaning all kinds of consciousness) to "I exist" (namely, as a soul), so Locke saw consciousness as evidence for soul — but a soul characterized only by conscious or rational states. Hence the problem. I suspect his Puritan upbringing had defined the image of God in the human person as reason, as, of course, theology has often done. But if the image of God makes us the persons we are and that image is simply a rational consciousness, then personal identity is simply a matter of continued consciousness. But if the image of God in us is more than reason, then we have further insight into personal identity.

I take seriously the suggestion of Karl Barth and others that *imago dei*

11. See C. Stephen Evans, *Preserving the Person* (Downers Grove, Ill.: InterVarsity Press, 1977), and Mary Van Leeuwen, *The Person in Psychology: A Contemporary Christian Appraisal* (Grand Rapids: Eerdmans, 1985).

means that we are not isolated consciousnesses but *relational* beings who find our identity in relation to other persons, to the natural world of which we are part, and to God himself, and that we are *responsible agents* in all these relationships. This finds support, I think, in the phenomenological account Martin Buber gives in *I and Thou,* and in other spin-offs from Hegel's famous "master-servant" dialectic. It is also developed in the work of Stanley Hauerwas on character development. Hauerwas argues for the role of community in personal formation, for the importance of reading the story of that community as my own story. It is in relationship, in a community whose past gives meaning to its present (not in the past of an isolated consciousness, but the past of the community to whom I belong) that values are assimilated, that character is thereby formed, and on that basis that personal identity takes shape: not just continued consciousness, but relationships, community, values, and character are needed for meaningful personal identity.

This has tremendous implications for Christian higher education. Note that because personal identity is tied to relationships, values, and character formation, the question "Who am I?" is a question about belonging, about values and trust and belief.

Bloom's Prescription

What then should be said about Allan Bloom's *prescription* for the American mind? Granted the symptoms he has identified and granted my revision of his diagnosis, does his prescription give hope for a cure? The "only serious solution," he thinks, is a return to liberal education, by which he means the Great Books tradition of the University of Chicago. Those who take advantage of liberal education, he claims, have the greatest moral and intellectual effect on the nation. Bloom's vigorous, blunt advocacy of liberal education is positive and exciting.

After all, do not the humanities with their great ideas and issues preserve and transmit those values that have shaped not only the American mind but also Western culture as a whole? And it is surely of the greatest importance that our students understand the big questions and wrestle with the great minds of the past. Homer and Plato, Augustine and Shakespeare, Locke and Rousseau — these are our people, our roots, our story in this Western community to which we belong. We learn what they believed, what values they embody, and they force us to think for ourselves while we think along with them. There is no substitute for liberal education. No substitute, it is true, but is it sufficient? Is classical liberal learning enough of a remedy for value relativism, for the loss of a worldview, and for the lack of personal identity? I think not.

Consider the diversity of values those classics represent — not only the continuity but also the discontinuity in the Western tradition. Are the Homeric virtues consonant with biblical morality? Is Plato's conception of justice the same as John Locke's? Does the Greek aristocratic view of work coincide with the Protestant work ethic? Nor can we exclude from our canon of classics the Nietzsches and Webers who, according to Bloom, have caused all this trouble. Exposure to the classics is itself no cure for value relativism. Their diversity stimulates inquiry, and their disagreements may be less tolerant than a wishy-washy laissez-faire relativist would tolerate. But the diversity of values is the invariable premise for any relativist argument — lots of grist here for the educational mill, but no surefire cure.

Consider also the conflicting worldviews that the history of ideas embodies. Do all the great minds ground values in reality? The same values? The same concept of reality? Is nature all there is, autonomously, blindly decreeing what good ends we seek? Or is nature the wisely ordered creation of a good God? In the classics, naturalist and idealist worldviews compete, as is evident in Wordsworth's pantheism, Jefferson's deism, and Nietzsche's nihilism. Does liberal learning both demonstrate the need for a worldview and settle what worldview it should be? An array of philosophical pharmaceuticals are available indeed, but no surefire cure.

Consider the matter of personal identity. What is it to be human? What makes a person the person he or she is? What ideal shall I adopt for the "myself" I seek to find, or create, or become, or whatever is the proper case? Am I to be a Platonic philosopher king? a Roman Stoic? a Cartesian ghost in a machine? Or if literature is my thing, should I join Hamlet in exorcising my guilty spots, or dance with Wordsworth's daffodils, or stay marooned on Matthew Arnold's "Dover Beach" where the sea of faith, once full, now retreats down "the naked shingles of the world"? The classics, like humankind generally, are both the glory and the shame of the universe. Where in this mottled community of glory and shame do I belong? That is still the question for personal identity. And where does my identity as a Christian come in?

The idea of a Christian college speaks to this contemporary mind because it speaks to the human condition. In contrast to value-free science and value-free education, and instead of accepting the value relativism of our day, the Christian college committed to biblical values has a mandate for moral education. In an academic environment of ever-increasing scientific specialization that too easily bypasses the larger questions of worldview, the Christian college rooted in a historic Christian view of things is mandated to articulate a worldview that grounds its values in the realities we confess. And in an age of individualists who seek to do their own things in their own separate ways in an endless search for personal identity and fulfillment, the Christian college can model the Christian community through the ages, where those who by faith belong, develop character, and find identity in relationship to God and his people in this world. That task is the mandate of Christian higher education.

The Opening of the Christian Mind

The mission of a Christian college in any society at any juncture in history is the opening of the Christian mind. Different denominations may rightly have different emphases within this overall mission, depending on their theological distinctives. For instance, I think of Wesleyan colleges that stress inner holiness as the wellspring of Christian thought and practice, of Mennonite institutions that emphasize peaceable service in a suffering world, of Reformed colleges that appeal to the cultural mandate under the sovereignty of God, and so forth. But common to us all is, or should be, the opening of the Christian mind.

As educators we seek an openness to learning and personal growth, to the world of ideas, the arts and sciences, the heritage of the past, the problems of the present, and the promise of the future; openness to cultural and social responsibility, openness to thinking for oneself and to acting in an informed and responsible manner, openness to saying and doing things in new and better ways. And as *Christian* educators we want it to be an openness to *thinking* and *acting* Christianly and being more *consistently* Christian in every department of learning and of life, an openness to God and the gospel in both the content and the process of education. We want Christianity to be seen and heard as a serious option for the contemporary mind, and we want the impact of a Christian ethic to be felt in business, government, the professions, and the family, as well, of course, as in the church; and we think that college can contribute to that end.

This opening of the Christian mind is what over the past years some of us have been calling the integration of faith, learning, and life. It goes beyond a loose conjunction of education and piety, or simply education "in a Christian environment," and especially any anti-intellectual disjunction of the type Richard Niebuhr characterized as "Christ against culture." Yet integration is obviously an ideal that is fully achieved only by God himself in his perfect understanding and in the faithfulness of his activity. For our colleges it is a goal; for teachers and administrators it is a lifelong struggle to see things whole, to think and become more consistently what we profess. Unfortunately, too often we settle for less than the possible, settle for a looser linkage of faith and learning, for only a half-open Christian mind.

Integration applies to the presuppositions on which Christian higher education rests, to our institutional and departmental objectives, and to the objectives of my courses as a teacher. It applies to curricular development and content, and therefore to faculty development, expectations, and programs. If science is not presuppositionless and learning is not value-free, then integration affects the methodology of the disciplines, and it influences the methodology of the teacher as well as his/her manner with students. In student development work, Christianity must be integrated with developmental psychology. The management theories and styles that administrators adopt should be deeply affected by Christian concepts of stewardly service, of equal justice for all, and of love. All this is but the opening of the Christian mind to what is rightly expected of Christian higher education.

But I want to move beyond these generalities to ask more directly how this mission of the Christian college addresses those three symptoms to which Bloom directs our attention. How well does the idea of a Christian college measure up to these challenges? Is the so-called integration of faith and learning on target for the American collegiate mind? Does it promise to open the mind where it matters? The three symptoms in question, again, are (1) value relativism, (2) the loss of a worldview that grounds values in reality, and (3) the lack of personal identity. My thesis is that the presuppositions of Christian higher education and the consequent integration of faith with learning directly address these symptoms, and that they do so not *per accidens,* by some fortuitous accident or clever *ad hoc* adjustment, but *per se,* by the very nature of the animal. The presuppositions I have in mind concern (1) the objectivity of values, (2) the theocentric unity of truth, and (3) the nature of persons.

The Objectivity of Values

Consider first the objectivity of values. Values are ideals, good ends we ought to prize and pursue. They are of various kinds: not only moral values, but also political values like equal justice for all, intellectual values like truth and understanding, aesthetic values like beauty, economic values like having the necessities of life, social values like friendship, psychological values like happiness, and religious values like knowing God. All of life comes value-laden, laden, that is, with possibilities for good.

These values I have named are not arbitrarily imposed on things by us, but rather they inhere in their respective aspects of life: thus, one value intrinsic to intellectual activity is understanding; one value intrinsic to art is beauty; one value intrinsic to religion (the major one, in fact) is knowing God. These values, then, are objective, not relative to the individual or the occasion; in some particular form or other they appear in every culture. The Christian regards them as God-given potentials for human existence; they are good to pursue because God made us the kind of beings we are in this kind of world he has created. So we want our students to love learning, to seek justice, to cherish friendships, to love God, and so forth. The objectivity of such values makes them a proper concern of education. Ernest Boyer contends that the study of a college major must be enriched with related requirements in the history of that field, its socio-economic implications, and the ethical issues it raises. If a major cannot be discussed in these terms, he adds, "it belongs in a trade school."[12]

In teaching such values a range of possible objectives present themselves: consciousness raising, consciousness sensitizing, values analysis, values clarification, values criticism, moral reasoning skills, moral imagi-

---

12. Ernest L. Boyer, *College: The Undergraduate Experience in America* (New York: Harper and Row, 1988), p. 110.

113

nation, moral decision-making, behavioral change, and character formation. While the first three or four of these objectives do not necessarily take us beyond value relativism, they clearly move in that direction. Values analysis, for instance, uncovers the values implicit in an account of people's choices and behavior, and in the alternative possibilities they present us.[13] It is a natural technique in teaching literature, history, or current issues in the social sciences. Values clarification does the same kind of thing with oneself. The natural outcome is values criticism, where judgments are made about the adequacy of the values that were actually pursued. Once reasons are given for the judgments we make, values criticism becomes not just an expression of personal taste and feeling but an appeal to something objective, something anybody in the case should have considered. Moral reasoning skills do this more methodically in their application of overarching ethical principles such as we find in philosophical and theological ethics.

Yet it is important to realize that moral decisions require more input than simply an awareness of the facts in a case, plus some overarching deontological or utilitarian principle like justice or love. Other background beliefs of a normative sort also come into play, and for the integration of faith and learning it is crucial that they be overt, explicit. Sexual ethics calls for a biblical understanding of human sexuality and its place and purpose in God's creation. Business ethics requires a clearheaded theology of work as stewardship of creation and service to others, in contrast to the Romanticist view of work as creative fulfillment, its Marxist counterpoint, or the acquisitiveness characteristic of our society today.

Background beliefs of this sort, what in another context Nicholas Wolterstorff has called "control beliefs,"[14] are so essential to consistently Christian thought that every academic department needs to ask itself what are the background beliefs that bear on its subject matter, and then to explore them in a biblical and theological perspective. What does biblical theology suggest about the purpose of government, about wealth and poverty, about play and beauty, about the purpose of punishment,

13. I refer you here to the helpful account in Richard L. Morrill, *Teaching Values in College: Facilitating Development of Ethical, Moral, and Values Awareness in Students* (San Francisco: Jossey-Bass, 1980).

14. See Nicholas Wolterstorff, *Reason Within the Bounds of Religion* (Grand Rapids: Eerdmans, 1976), pp. 11-16.

etc.? And how do these conceptions affect policies and concrete decisions in those areas? This, I maintain, is an essential beginning for the opening of the Christian mind.

The objectives of value education go beyond reasoning skills and moral decision-making to behavioral change and character formation. My point is that Christianity presupposes the objectivity of values and, as Bloom points out, so do many classical non-Christian approaches. Value education in the Christian college plainly must reach beyond value relativism and work toward thoughtful Christian value commitments. This is not indoctrination, which would merely revert the student to Perry's earlier stage of unthinking, dogmatic dualism. It is rather value *education* in that it moves beyond both relativism and dogmatism to self-critical and thoughtful commitment.

Theocentric Unity of Truth

A second presupposition of Christian higher education is the theocentric unity of truth. By this, I mean first that all the truth in various areas of learning is in principle an interrelated whole, and second that the truth about everything relates to God. The ultimate unity of truth is perhaps a truism, but it is an important one because otherwise no overall worldview would even be conceivable, and there would be no real *uni*-verse but only a fragmented *multi*-verse endlessly at variance with itself, marking the end of all coherent thought and action. But the second part, that it all relates to God, needs more elaboration.

All truth about anything in any and every discipline, about everything past, present, or future, everything possible in history, art, technology, or creative thought, is about some aspect of God's creation or something God has thought but never created. It all relates to his being, his wisdom, his purposes in creating or not creating whatever he did or did not make. It is not only that all truth is known perfectly to him, nor only that all the truth we ever know is ultimately thanks to him, but that it is all about him and his activity in creation. Our disciplines relate to each other by virtue of the way God made everything in this *uni*verse of his, just as they hold the value possibilities they do by virtue of the way he made things. There is a theocentric unity of truth. In the practice of human understanding, we are still learning, we see through a glass darkly, and we know only in part. But in confessing that by him and for him and

115

through him are all things, we confess in principle that of which in practice we still strain for a closer view.

This presupposition directly addresses the second of Bloom's symptoms, the loss of any ground for values in reality. The theocentric unity of truth grounds values in God himself, the values involved in his creative activity. The Genesis refrain echoes repeatedly: "It was good . . . it was good . . . it was very good." So it is God's values, his good ends for this world of his, that we are to prize and pursue. The Christian worldview grounds values in the reality of God, his creation, and his redemption.

It has broader educational implications as well. If the theocentric unity of truth is taken seriously, there can be no dichotomy of sacred and secular learning that deprecates secular subjects as if they were unrelated to God and therefore unimportant, or worse still, an inherently dangerous "wisdom of this world." Critical discernment we all need, of course, but we need it within the sanctity of biblical studies as well as the secularity of psychology or philosophy.

The unity of truth speaks also to curricular integration. To tell the physicist or mathematician to relate her subject matter to other disciplines is hardly necessary. To ask her to relate it to God will not produce much beyond a reaffirmation of the wisdom and power of the Creator. But if we try to address curricular integration in terms of the theocentric unity of truth, then some sort of general education pattern begins to emerge that requires work in Bible, theology, and philosophy — and ethics if we are addressing the grounding of values in reality. For it is in these disciplines — in the case of the physicist, a theology of nature, a philosophy of science, and an environmental ethic — that we best uncover the interrelatedness.

This is why integration is sometimes said to involve "foundational" thinking, for it is in the theoretical foundations of science, education, or ethics that the most basic differences between Christian and non-Christian worldviews arise. So, we have to think critically about contemporary philosophy of science, philosophy of education, and theories of literary criticism. We need to take a hard look at deconstructionism and what it says about truth, human knowledge, and language — and, at the other extreme, to keep a wary eye on persistent positivist tendencies in some of the behavioral sciences. Epistemological questions will be crucial in overcoming scientific exclusivism. Assumptions about human nature will be critical as well as the orderedness of nature and the objectivity and ground of values. What are the assumptions currently operative in the various disciplines? Are they consonant with a Christian view of things? What is their logical basis? What are their implications? Uncovering and scrutinizing foundational presuppositions is a major part of what I have called "worldview analysis," and it belongs in every major in the college.[15]

Another key ingredient of worldview analysis is the more constructive work of articulating a Christian worldview and tracing its implications for the various disciplines. I suggest this is a threefold job. First, it involves spelling out the contours of that worldview. The second job is to bring these broad perspectives to the large foundational questions I have mentioned, epistemological and methodological questions, questions about the nature of reality, its orderedness and the causes at work, and questions about the nature and basis of value. The third job is a more focused application of Christian perspectives to particular concepts within the discipline, like the "background beliefs" that inform moral decisions. A theology of work should be informing not only business ethics, but also studies generally in business, economics, and sociology, as well as the career guidance our schools nowadays offer. By the same token we need a theology of the family, a theology of art, of play, and of competition, a theology of the intellect, of the environment, of government, of friendship . . . you name it. These are not the theological topics that seminarians usually study, but they are the ones our colleges need to explore.

We have to think theologically in constructing and articulating a Christian worldview. Each department could profitably hold a series of faculty colloquia exploring how Christian theology touches its area of inquiry. One Presbyterian college actually requires each faculty candidate for tenure to write a paper on how the Westminster Confession of Faith relates to his or her academic field. And then there are the curricular and pedagogical questions to answer: Where and how will our majors become involved in this sort of thinking? Even when this is said and done there is, as we all know, no guarantee that a person will think and

15. You can see such worldview analysis at work in an excellent collection of essays: David Wolfe and Harold Heie, eds., *The Reality of Christian Learning* (Grand Rapids: Eerdmans, 1987).

act Christianly, and here another presupposition of Christian higher education comes into play.

The Nature of Persons

This third presupposition is about the nature of persons. Indeed, it illustrates rather well the critical role of foundational beliefs in any discipline. We are talking education, where one of the foundational beliefs in any philosophy of education will be the operative view of a person. John Dewey's educational approach assumes that a person is a sociobiological organism adjusting to problem situations in the process of natural selection. Classical education assumed we are primarily rational beings whose contemplative understanding governs all we do. How for educational purposes shall we characterize a Christian doctrine of the person?

My way of doing it is to say (1) we are *relational beings,* by virtue of our essential relatedness to the natural world (we are of the dust of the earth), to other persons (it is not good to be alone), and to God (whose nature we image); (2) we are *responsible agents* in all these relationships; and (3) we are profoundly and pervasively affected by our condition in *sin* and *grace.* Immediately the contrast stands out with the picture of egocentric individualism Robert Bellah and his associates painted in *Habits of the Heart.*[16] For the Bible sees us as individuals *in community,* and certain kinds of community as divinely ordained by virtue of the kinds of beings God has made us humans to be. Family, the economic community, and the political unit, theologians tell us, are natural, created orders, law spheres, mandates . . . the terminology varies.

Now how does this bear on Bloom's third symptom, the lack of personal identity? When we discussed that symptom, I suggested that the empiricists' discussions of personal identity concentrated on the continuity of consciousness in one's memory because of their operative assumption that the person is most basically a conscious, rational being. In contrast, nineteenth- and twentieth-century European philosophy saw affective dimensions of personality as at least as basic as the rational, and perhaps more so. I think of Hegel's master-servant relationship, of the immediacy of interpersonal awareness in Heidegger's *Mit-*

---

16. See Robert N. Bellah, et al., *Habits of the Heart: Individualism and Commitment in American Life* (Berkeley: University of California Press, 1985).

sein, of Buber's "I-Thou" being prior to just the "I," of Edith Stein on empathy and Max Scheler on sympathy. Self-consciousness, on this kind of account, is not individualistic but relational, interpersonal, a product of social existence, of shared bodily and emotional experience. Personal identity arises in relationship, in community, not in solitary confinement like Robinson Crusoe alone on his island — even Crusoe had his goats and his God!

I find this alternative account much closer to the biblical than to that of the empiricists. Personal identity in the Old Testament is found in being the *son* of so-and-so, of the *tribe* of such-and-such, in the *land* of Israel, into which Jehovah God brought us. Identity is relational. Our surnames still bear witness to this sort of thing: John-*son,* Hender-*son* or Golds-*borough,* or even *Smith* or *Taylor* (indicating our trades). All this bears witness, American individualism notwithstanding, that individualism — rooted in enlightenment, science, and empiricism — is one of the operative assumptions of our society that Christians must question. God made us to be biologically, economically, intellectually, and emotionally interdependent with our destinies intertwined.

What then can the Christian college contribute to personal identity in this age of individualism? An understanding of the historical roots of individualism and its problems? It can surely provide this, but even more important for personal growth will be entrance into relationships, community, and heritage. If we are at heart relational beings, then relationships in which we identify with a community and its heritage are essential. And while a Christian community can in measure model what responsible participation in relationship to nature, other persons, and God can be, it will be more than a model if one is genuinely a member of that community, part of its life and part of the action.

And we foster the development of relationships, community, and heritage in part through relating stories that help ground identity. For example, we have our stories about America that feed our sense of national identity. We have the biblical story, the history of the church, the heritage of Christian scholars and leaders through the centuries on which we purport to build, the stories of those faithful ones who founded and led our institutions in the past, and the stories that grow up around popular, fabled professors on your campus and mine. Campus life has many dimensions: athletics, residence halls, bull sessions, student pranks, service projects, internships, debates, even tragedies. These are part of the life of community. The kind of story they tell, the kind of community they build, influences the kind of personal identity our students will have.

I remember talking some years ago with a Yale professor who had been trying to figure out what made some of his graduate students who came from small Christian colleges such good philosophers. He had gone incognito to Calvin College in Michigan and wandered the campus for a couple of days, trying to figure it out. He said he came up with two things: having a defined theological heritage, they had already learned to spot a conceptual problem when they saw one; and a sense of community, academic and religious, gave them personal identity within the larger academic world.

What community contributes to personal growth and personal identity has to do also with character development — the last of those ten objectives for value education — for we are valuing beings, responsible agents. Character development is the development of personal identity through the solidification of values in inner dispositions that define who I am and how I will therefore conduct myself in the various relationships of life. The work of Stanley Hauerwas makes plain the role of community and its story in imparting values and shaping moral character, and so contributing to personal identity.

But let us not jump to the conclusion that the academic dimensions of these college years contribute nothing to personal identity. On the contrary, a liberal learning that explores the cultural heritage is telling the story of the larger community of which we are part. The student whose imagination is captured, who identifies empathetically with that heritage, will find its ideals solidifying in his character and giving him personal identity.

By the same token, if we want our students to identify with the Third World, then we must expose them to the heritage of those other cultures. And if we want them to think Christianly, we must lead them into dialogue with other Christian thinkers and the history of Christian thought. If we want them to achieve a distinctively Christian identity in today's world, we will see to it that they explore the exciting story of the Christian presence in this world — serving, suffering, thinking, reforming. This sort of thing is the real point in what Bloom and others say about the importance of the liberal arts in teaching values. A liberal arts education is about our story, it is the heritage of a community and its culture, but it takes imagination, empathy, excitement, and love of learning, not just detached intellectualization, for the liberal arts to make their full contribution to personal growth.

Our presupposition about persons as relational beings has other implications as well. It will affect the behavioral and social sciences. It will help define the kinds of skills and personal qualities we want our graduates to exhibit as the people God made them to be. But I rest my case for the Christian college on the argument that these presuppositions of Christian higher education (the objectivity of values, the theocentric unity of truth, the nature of persons), and the kind of integration they imply for faith, learning, and campus life, speak directly to the troubling tendencies of today's students.

For the problems of today are at heart the human problem to which the gospel in its fullness speaks. We lose our full identity as humans when our values are all at sea, no longer grounded in the reality of our Creator, his creative work, and redeeming love. The mandate of the Christian college is to reintegrate what has fallen apart, to reunify faith, learning, and life. In a word, our call is to open a genuinely Christian mind.

QUESTIONS FOR REFLECTION AND DISCUSSION

1. To what extent are the three symptoms that Holmes discusses (value relativism, loss of a worldview to ground values, and lack of personal identity) evident among your students?

2. Holmes lays heavy blame for these problems at the feet of modern science, with its hard-and-fast separation of facts and values. Beyond the Christian critique he offers of modern science, what further resources might be offered by the last half-century's developments in epistemology and the philosophy of science?

3. On Holmes's account, Bloom's solution — a healthy dose of classical liberal education grounded in the great texts — is a necessary but insufficient response to the plight of contemporary students. What merits and limits arise from a great texts–based education of the sort endorsed by Bloom? From the sort endorsed by Holmes, that takes seriously the normative commitments of Christianity? How should the great texts be read and taught in a Christian college or university?

4. In what ways is your teaching and scholarship shaped by the Christian presuppositions identified by Holmes: the objectivity of values, the theocentric unity of truth, and the nature of persons? How are these presuppositions reflected in your institution's liberal education core? In its various majors? In its professional education programs?

FURTHER RELATED WORK BY THIS AUTHOR

Holmes, Arthur F., ed. *The Making of a Christian Mind: A Christian World View and the Academic Enterprise.* Grand Rapids: Eerdmans, 1985.

Holmes, Arthur F. *The Idea of a Christian College.* Grand Rapids: Eerdmans, 1987.

———. *Shaping Character: Moral Education in the Christian College.* Grand Rapids: Eerdmans, 1991.

———. *Fact, Value, and God.* Grand Rapids: Eerdmans, 1997.

———. *Building the Christian Academy.* Grand Rapids: Eerdmans, 2001.

Chapter Eight

Christian Higher Education and the Conversion of the West

DENTON LOTZ

Overlooking Lenin Hills near Moscow University, there is a little Russian Orthodox chapel that I visited many years ago. I asked the guide if it was open, and she replied, "Ne rebotayet" — it doesn't work. I went to the chapel anyway and knocked on the door. After several minutes a young Orthodox deacon came out to greet me. He was wearing a long black robe, had a long beard, and his face was filled with a saintly look of deep joy. As he showed me the church, I asked him how he became a Christian. An amazing story of faith unfolded. Three years previously he had been a Marxist professor of philosophy at the Lenin Institute. He said, "One day, whether you are an atheist or not, you have to make a decision whether there is a God." He related a dream he had one night, and an experience of Christ as Lord. The next day he read the Gospels and committed himself to the Christian faith. Of course, he was dismissed from his teaching position as well as from the Party. His family disowned him. But now he was joyful because he had found true meaning in life. I asked him, "What about the future of the Christian faith in the Soviet Union?" His eyes lit up as he said, "The future belongs to us. In the nineteenth century we had the peasants and lost the intellectuals.

This chapter was presented for the H. I. Hester Lecture Series at the June 1987 ASBCS meeting, and adapted for this collection from the September 1987 issue of *The Southern Baptist Educator.*

But in the twentieth century we have lost the peasants and regained the intellectuals, and one day all of Russia will again be Christian!"

This brief conversation left a deep impression upon me, particularly when after fifteen years as a missionary in Eastern Europe, I returned to the United States. In observing the American scene at colleges and universities, it became obvious to me that precisely the opposite had happened in the United States. In the twentieth century we have lost the intellectuals but have the peasants. The consequences of this loss spell a dreary future for the Christian faith, if we cannot reverse it. Basically, America's intelligentsia have rejected the Christian faith. Those institutions founded upon the belief that all truth is ultimately related to God's revelation in Jesus Christ are very often hostile even to a religious interpretation of their history. If the Russian Orthodox deacon was optimistic about the future of Christianity in his country because of the regaining of the intellectuals, we American Christians should stand in utter fear at the loss of our intellectuals.

Can the West be converted? Can Western civilization, the fruit of Christian theology and biblical faith, be brought back into the fold of the Christian tradition? This is the significant question that we, as missionaries and evangelists, would address to leaders in Christian higher education. The question is stated eloquently by Bishop Lesslie Newbigin, formerly Bishop of the Church of South India, in a seminal book entitled *Foolishness to the Greeks: The Gospel and Western Culture,* his 1984 Warfield Lectures at Princeton Theological Seminary.[1] It is the missiological question for all of us living in the West. For too long we have coasted along, not realizing that an underlying philosophy of the faith has long been eliminated from our institutions of higher learning and that what we have is a vestige of Christianity with no intellectual defense at the very heart of the American educational system.

There can be many defenses and reasons for having Christian colleges. We can speak of morality and rules, of Christian environment and worship and passing on the tradition, but I believe if there is any reason for a Christian college or university today, it must essentially be rooted in a missiological context. That is, the existence of a Christian college has as an essential reason for being the reclamation of the mind of our country

1. Lesslie Newbigin, *Foolishness to the Greeks: The Gospel and Western Culture* (Grand Rapids: Eerdmans, 1986).

for Christ, which has been lost in the secularization of the American educational system. It has a missionary responsibility to convert a lost and godless generation of searching students to a biblical worldview. The Christian college must serve the church in its communication of the truth of Christ to a decadent and frivolous society whose so-called search for truth has ended on a garbage heap of humankind's sinful inadequacy without God. In short, a fundamental purpose of Christian higher education must be the conversion of the West. How shall we proceed?

Understanding Where We Are and How We Got Here

Newbigin offers a brilliant analysis of Western culture that helps us understand as Christians — and more significantly as educators — where we are and how we got here from the point of view of a modern Christian philosophy of history and science. Basically, Newbigin argues, the problem is that following Francis Bacon (and the ensuing Enlightenment-based scientific worldview), scholars saw their task as one of scientifically answering, in terms of cause and effect, the question "How?" The Greek and Christian question prior to the Enlightenment was always a question of purpose, "Why?" Thus we have the gradual division that has become a chasm today between the "how" of science and the "why" of theology. Science sees everything in terms of cause and effect. Theology interprets reality in terms of purpose. For scientific, post-Enlightenment thinkers, God is excluded from explanations, since they are not concerned with purpose but only with explanations of cause and effect. Newbigin states that this dichotomy between science and theology can be summarized as the common separation today of "fact" and "value." "Facts" are the domain of science, neutral and acceptable to all. Thus, the public domain is concerned only with facts. On the other hand, "values" are personal matters, left to the individual or the church, but not to be pushed into the public domain because there are many values, all of which should be tolerated. So, Newbigin writes, "In the physics classroom the student learns what the 'facts' are and is expected at the end to believe the truth of what he has learned. In the religious education classroom he is invited to choose what he likes best."[2]

2. Newbigin, *Foolishness to the Greeks*, p. 39.

125

The consequences for Christian education have been enormous. In opting for this distinction between "public facts" and "private values," we lost a battle to significantly shape education. Newbigin writes, "Having been badly battered in its encounter with modern science, Christianity in its Protestant form has largely accepted relegation to the private sector, where it can influence the choice of values by those who take this option. By doing so, it has secured for itself a continuing place, at the cost of surrendering the crucial field."[3] In this way, the church can grow in its private sphere, and we can have government leaders defend religion in general, but at the cost of marginalization. For example, Eisenhower made the innocuous claim of America's need for a religious faith, ". . . and I don't care what it is."[4]

What has been the effect, then, of this separation of facts and values upon the public domain, including education? Again Newbigin suggests, "The awesome claim . . . of Jesus Christ to be alone the Lord of all the world, the light that alone shows the whole of reality as it really is, the life that alone endures forever — this claim is effectively silenced."[5] Look at the "public world" of television, where 85 percent of American television producers, according to some polls, are either unchurched or anti-church. Study the curriculum of the secular university or the public schools. Newbigin states that students in our public schools must know that "the development of the individual person is governed by the program in the DNA molecule . . . [but that] every human being is made to glorify God and enjoy Him forever is an opinion held by some people but not part of public truth."[6]

Not only Christian thinkers such as Newbigin see the tragic consequences that the separation of facts and values has brought upon the university, but classical scholars like Allan Bloom also have joined the chorus of serious thinkers depressed about the present situation in institutions of higher learning. In *The Closing of the American Mind,* Bloom writes:

> . . . the crisis of liberal education is a reflection of a crisis at the peaks of learning, an incoherence and incompatibility among the first prin-

3. Newbigin, *Foolishness to the Greeks,* p. 19.
4. Quoted in Peter L. Berger, *Facing Up to Modernity* (New York: Basic Books, 1977), p. 155.
5. Newbigin, *Foolishness to the Greeks,* p. 19.
6. Newbigin, *Foolishness to the Greeks,* p. 38.

ciples with which we interpret the world, an intellectual crisis of the greatest magnitude, which constitutes the crisis of our civilization. But perhaps it would be true to say that the crisis consists not so much in this incoherence but in our incapacity to discuss or even recognize it. Liberal education flourished when it prepared the way for the discussion of a unified view of nature and man's place in it, which the best minds debated on the highest level. It decayed when what lay beyond it were only specialties, the premises of which do not lead to any such vision.[7]

Moreover, in the name of tolerance, students today do not even have the alternative of asking religious questions. Bloom states that "a serious life means being fully aware of the alternatives, thinking about them with all the intensity one brings to bear on life-and-death questions, in full recognition that every choice is a great risk with necessary consequences that are hard to bear."[8] The Marxist scholar in Moscow realized the consequences of these alternatives and took the risk, read the Bible, and his life was changed. Do students in America's institutions of higher learning have the opportunity even to be confronted with the choice of reading the Bible? As Bloom says:

> God was slowly executed here; it took two hundred years, but local theologians tell us He is now dead. His place has been taken by the sacred. Love was put to death by the psychologists. Its place has been taken by sex and meaningful relationships. That has taken only about seventy-five years. It should not be surprising that a new science, thanatology, or death with dignity, is on the way to putting death to death.[9]

On and on one could go listing the deficiencies of our modern educational system and the dilemmas caused by our pragmatism, which "saw the past as radically imperfect and regarded our history as irrelevant or as a hindrance to rational analysis of our present."[10] This ignorance of our culture, our history, and our society is also an ignorance of religion.

7. Allan Bloom, *The Closing of the American Mind* (New York: Simon and Schuster, 1987), pp. 346-47.

8. Bloom, *The Closing of the American Mind,* p. 227.

9. Bloom, *The Closing of the American Mind,* p. 230.

10. Bloom, *The Closing of the American Mind,* p. 56.

As a result, "real religion and knowledge of the Bible have diminished to the vanishing point," says Bloom.[11] We credit all of this so-called progress to a scientific worldview based upon a rational analysis of the facts. Reinhold Niebuhr criticized modern educators, saying, "Modern educators are, like rationalists of all the ages, too enamored of the function of reason in life. The world of history, particularly in man's collective behavior, will never be conquered by reason, unless reason uses tools, and is itself driven by forces which are not rational."[12]

Christian educators and Christian colleges, in the midst of this culture, must rediscover and reassert the purpose of Christian higher education. They must not only dialogue with modern secular education, but also seek its conversion for the good of the church and the nation. And the culture in which this work takes place in many respects is aptly described as a neo-pagan society. Indeed, we have moved beyond a merely secular society to a pagan society that denies God and has its own idols and own pantheon of new gods, whether in music, art, film, or literature. It is therefore the task of Christian higher education to prepare the groundwork for the conversion of this neo-pagan society.

Issues for Christian Higher Education in a Neo-Pagan Society

W. A. Visser 't Hooft has been one of the formative thinkers and leaders of the World Council of Churches since its inception in 1948. In 1975, Visser 't Hooft wrote a significant article titled "Evangelism in the Neo-Pagan Situation." He claims, "Evangelism is in the first place the transmission of God's question to humanity. And that question is and remains whether we are willing to accept Jesus Christ as the one and only Lord of life."[13] But then he goes on and says, "But I believe that we must try to relate God's question to the existential situation of people and show that as they answer God's question they find at the same time the

11. Bloom, *The Closing of the American Mind,* p. 56.
12. Reinhold Niebuhr, *Moral Man and Immoral Society: A Study in Ethics and Politics* (New York: Charles Scribner's, 1932), pp. xv-xvi.
13. W. A. Visser 't Hooft, "Evangelism in the NeoPagan Situation," in *Mission Trends No. 2: Evangelization,* ed. Gerald H. Anderson and Thomas F. Stransky (New York: Paulist Press, 1975), p. 123.

answer to their deepest concerns."[14] Visser 't Hooft sees the questions of modern humanity as threefold — concerning nature, sex, and human justice. If Christian educational institutions are going to be successful in educating students for Christian witness in a neo-pagan society, then we need to face these questions and enable students to confront them in our society.

Creation

Yearly on June 21, thousands of young Britishers gather around Stonehenge to celebrate the summer solstice. Recently, the event was sponsored by the Pagan Society for Peace. Although this is only a small group, paganism as a philosophy is alive and well in our society. In an article titled "Europe's Neo-Paganism: A Perverse Inculturation," Marc Spindler writes that "the time when 'paganism' was a dirty word is over and I am able to quote a number of recent European writers using the term 'paganism' in a favorable way, affirming 'the genius of paganism,' its capacity to offer a valid alternative to Christianity."[15] A French writer describes it this way, "Paganism seeks religion in our exalted feeling of wholeness here and now. Far from desacralizing the world, it sacralizes it. Indeed: it takes the world for sacred."[16]

Biblical faith affirms the creation of the world and humankind as stewards thereof. A misinterpretation of the Old Testament has often led to a laissez-faire attitude toward the earth, and we sometimes have not taken seriously our responsibility to reverence God's creation. The Christian teacher must show that a return to nature worship will not overcome our present predicament, but that "rediscovering the meaning of Creation and . . . treating nature as a gift of God" will overcome it.[17] A Christian view of creation enables us to see that the destruction of the earth's resources and the accumulation of more and more is counter to biblical faith. Psalm 8, which depicts the beauty of creation and humanity's dominion over it, is not a call for destruction but preservation: "Thou hast given him dominion over the work of thy hands; thou hast

14. Visser 't Hooft, "Evangelism in the NeoPagan Situation," p. 123.

15. Marc R. Spindler, "Europe's Neo-Paganism: A Perverse Inculturation," *International Bulletin of Missionary Research* (January 1987): 8.

16. Spindler, "Europe's Neo-Paganism," p. 9.

17. Visser 't Hooft, "Evangelism in the NeoPagan Situation," p. 124.

put all things under his feet. . . ." The dominion given to humankind is no excuse for desecration.

Chuck Colson tells of being at an airport and waiting for a rental car. The young man ahead of him was very upset that he could not get a white Lincoln Continental; only a black one was available. Emblazoned on his T-shirt was the phrase, "The one who dies with the most toys wins." Unfortunately, this is the attitude many have toward creation. We want more and more and do not see what we have as a gift of God, not ours to own but rather to receive graciously and use in service to God. Christian scholars — not at the seminary level alone, but in the arts and sciences of our colleges — must develop a theology of creation adequate to confront the challenge of paganism and other sub-Christian views of the earth.

Sex

If ever there were a need for a Christian theology of sexuality able to confront the pagan sexual culture of today, there is now. Allan Bloom eloquently summarizes the situation: "Freud made it possible to consider sexual repression a medical complaint, and therefore endowed it with the prestige automatically enjoyed by anything having to do with health in a nation devoted to self-preservation."[18] Much modern rock music builds on this premise in a way that our youth lose all sense of guilt or shame against the misuse of sex. The words in pagan rock music, says Bloom, "implicitly and explicitly describe bodily acts that satisfy sexual desire and treat them as its only natural and routine culmination for children who do not yet have the slightest imagination of love, marriage, or family."[19]

Here we are confronted with a blatant and vulgar denigration of the Christian view of sex. It is a sad situation when teenagers of eighteen years of age are already burned out sexually. If the church devalued Eros, paganism has made him its new god. Christian teachers must be able to show that the biblical understanding of sex is one of "Eros saved by Agape," as Denis de Rougemont says.[20] Visser 't Hooft maintains that we need to show that the biblical concept of faithfulness does not destroy

---

18. Bloom, *The Closing of the American Mind,* p. 233.
19. Bloom, *The Closing of the American Mind,* p. 74.
20. Visser 't Hooft, "Evangelism in the NeoPagan Situation," p. 124.

sex but makes it possible to enjoy it to its limits in a structure of freedom and discipline before God and one's partner.[21]

There is no excuse for a Christian college to compromise on this issue. Christian administrators, faculty, and students must be encouraged to show the positive and beautiful sexuality made possible by faith. There is no call for a return to a negative view of sex but to an affirmation of God's creation within the monogamous family, where true sexuality and freedom are experienced. Virginity before marriage and chastity in marriage are not Christian options but the Christian obligation.

Human Justice

Visser 't Hooft concludes his list of modern humanity's questions with the statement, "No modern evangelist will really speak to the condition of the present generation unless he relates his message to the issues of human justice."[22] No Christian can rightly escape into otherworldly spirituality. We must confront the question of justice today, which includes questions of war and peace, wealth and poverty, employment and unemployment, and the like.

Douglas Waruta, president of the Baptist Seminary in Arusha, Tanzania, was walking the streets of Baltimore and saw Kenyan coffee beans selling for five dollars a pound. He said, "I do not understand economics, but my mother picked those coffee beans in Kenya for fifteen cents a pound. Someone is stealing from my mother." Is it any wonder that when the gospel came to the developing countries, it also brought with it a sense of justice? Too often our faith in the West has been divorced from this holistic view of mission that our missionaries proclaimed with the gospel overseas. As a result, we have Christians here in the West, as caricatured by Karl Barth, who read either the Bible or the newspaper, when Barth said we actually need to have the Bible in one hand and the newspaper in the other.

If we are not involved in the struggle for justice, we should not be surprised when secular groups describe us as irrelevant. Christian education must prevent compartmentalization of faith. We need to hold both together, spirituality and justice, peace with God and peace with

21. Visser 't Hooft, "Evangelism in the NeoPagan Situation," p. 124.
22. Visser 't Hooft, "Evangelism in the NeoPagan Situation," p. 124.

the world. Manfred Brauch warned that if we do not hold faith and works together, "We can end up with a social gospel without a Saviour; a gospel of justice without Jesus; a gospel of political peace without the Prince of Peace; a gospel of bread for the world without the Bread of Life and a gospel of harmony in human relationships without a life-giving relationship to the Holy One."[23]

I am not suggesting that we should have a demonstration on campus every week for some cause of justice. On the contrary, students at a Christian college must be confronted in the classroom with the great Christian classics dealing with faith and its relationship to society. To read the prophets Amos and Isaiah or Jeremiah without relating them to our world today is escapism. Biblical faith that leads to conversion will confront the issues head-on with the convincing arguments of Scripture and the great Christian theologians throughout history.

The issues confronting Christian higher education vis-à-vis a pagan, non-believing world are more numerous than the three mentioned above. Students need to understand that slogans are not enough and that at the center of our search for education and knowledge is a loving God who sustains all. Without God, the world and all our involvement is meaningless. Helmut Thielicke warned German students of this, and his comments are appropriate for us:

> . . . the decisive issue is whether we can maintain the Christian West if we lose connections with the One who supports, quickens, and fulfills it. Is it possible to hold on to certain Christian ideas of humanity, love of the neighbor, and faith, when the figure of Jesus himself has disappeared and when, instead of the original, we hold only copies of copies in our hand? Is what remains anything more than the momentum of a machine whose motor has long since been turned off and whose own stopping is just a matter of time? Are we going to be able to sustain the thesis of "the infinite value of a human soul" when the basis for that value has disappeared: namely, that the soul has been dearly bought, that the Son of God died for it, and that it therefore lives under the patronage of an eternal goodness?[24]

23. "Teaching Is Manfred Brauch's First Love," *Eastern's World: News and Views of Eastern College and the Eastern Baptist Theological Seminary* (March 1985): 11.

24. Helmut Thielicke, *Being a Christian When the Chips Are Down*, trans. H. George Anderson (Philadelphia: Fortress Press, 1979), pp. 41-42.

Not to put too fine a point on it, then, we who embrace a commitment to a vocation in Christian higher education must also accept a commensurate commitment to our own conversion, individually and corporately. For if the Christian college is to lead the way in the conversion of the West, then it too needs conversion.

The Conversion of the Christian College

The West will never be converted until the college is converted. And the college will never be converted until there is a radical rediscovery of the unity of all truth in Jesus Christ. Conversion must not only be of the heart, but also must seek what the apostle Paul called "the mind of Christ" (Phil. 2:5). We must witness in all fields of academic endeavor that God has spoken, that the world has purpose and meaning, and that at one time there entered this planet in the form of a human being, God himself. In that person the world is called to change its mind, repent, be born anew, be converted. Those who have experienced this, Newbigin says, must use the language of testimony, "since this testimony, so far from being capable of validation by methods of modern science, provides itself with the foundation on which modern science rests, namely, the assurance that the world is both rational and contingent."[25]

In a Christian college this language of testimony must surely come from the administration, but even more obviously from the faculty. I remember speaking with Bishop Stephen Neill, asking how we could regain the university for Christ. He said we must begin with Christian faculty members; and if there aren't any, we need to convert some! Think of the tremendous Christian influence among students that C. S. Lewis had. The key to converting the college will be dedicated and committed faculty members who intellectually and morally are not only equal to their colleagues at secular universities, but in fact are leaders in the whole field of academia. The mind of Christ needs to express itself in excellence in the humanities or the sciences. We need to begin training the best and brightest, not only to be great thinkers, but to regard their intellectual work as a Christian vocation.

This will require repentance. The university, the church, and indi-

---

25. Newbigin, *Foolishness to the Greeks,* p. 94.

vidual Christians need to repent of our presumptions upon the mercies of God. We need to hear the word from Romans, "Do you not know that God's kindness is meant to lead you to repentance?" (Rom. 2:4). The first of Martin Luther's ninety-five theses is that the call of Christ is a daily call to repentance. The whole community of faith must confess to an unbelieving world that we have sought the power of the world more than the power of the resurrection. We have sought this world's wealth more than Christ's poverty. We have sought too much by reason to find God instead of opening ourselves to the God who finds us. And repenting, we will be open to a new vision of Christ as Lord of history and Lord of our lives. The West will only be converted when Christian colleges are converted and can offer the intellectual, philosophical, and spiritual basis for a new revival of learning and commitment to Jesus Christ. This is the decision before us. Paul Loeffler states the case precisely: "Christian education minus conversion is religiosity without decision."[26]

The Conversion of the Church —
Learning from the Church Overseas

If Christian colleges and universities must be based upon servanthood and responsibility to the church, the church must support the institutions that it founds sacrificially as a missionary enterprise, giving it the freedom that a Christian institution of higher learning requires. The church and the college exist in a creative tension. Generally the church requires discipline of the college and the college requires freedom of the church. Freedom and discipline cannot exist separately. It is in the tension of one with the other that true freedom and true discipline exist. After all, Helmut Thielicke insists that "freedom is possible only within certain limitations and a framework of obligations, if it is not to become a playground of neutral values and thus a force that produces mere chaos."[27] Thielicke goes on to show this in the story of the prodigal son. He concludes: "We have only to choose between bondage to the Father,

26. Paul Loeffler, "The Biblical Concept of Conversion," in *Mission Trends No. 2,* p. 42.

27. Helmut Thielicke, *The Freedom of the Christian Man: A Christian Confrontation with the Secular Gods,* trans. John W. Doberstein (New York: Harper and Row, 1963), p. 27.

which makes us free, and bondage to the powers of this world, which enslaves us. Only he who finds God finds himself."[28]

Part of the educational crisis in church-related institutions is that the church has not been willing to allow freedom and the college has not been willing to accept discipline. If the university requires conversion, it is no less true that the church also requires conversion. In fact, the sorry state of many church colleges can be laid directly at the door of the church, which has not repented of its medieval attempt to lord it over everyone with no repentance, no compassion, and no mercy. That the churches are still the number one segregated institution must say something about this lack of repentance and conversion on the part of wide areas of the church.

By way of telling, sharp, convicting contrast, a look at the church overseas, in a very different context, illustrates a servant church in an unbelieving world. Take, for example, China. In 1986 the Baptist World Alliance sponsored a tour to the People's Republic of China. Part of this world friendship tour was a conference in Nanjing, where leaders from around the world listened to Chinese Christian leaders, professors, and students. We did not go to instruct, to criticize, or to tell them how to do it. We went to listen. And what we heard was a remarkable testimony of the grace of God in the life of the church and its people. Again and again we heard how the church prior to the revolution was so Western that often it did not hear the cries of its own people. After the revolution and many years of persecution and suffering, it learned so to identify with its people that today the churches are crowded, as are the more than fourteen theological seminaries. Before the revolution in 1949, there were 700,000 Protestant Christians. By 2002, there were officially thirteen million Protestant Christians in post-denominational China, with estimates as high as seventy million additional members and friends in house churches. In 1979, at the end of the "Gang of Four" rule, there was only one church open in Shanghai, but by 2002 there were more than fourteen thousand churches open, with twenty thousand mission points across China. A new hymnal has been printed. A graduate theological seminary is producing syllabi and books for the people. Two churches are being opened every day. Thousands of young people are flooding the churches and asking, "What is the purpose of life?"

---

28. Thielicke, *The Freedom of the Christian Man,* p. 28.

We heard a beautiful testimony of a young man who during the Cultural Revolution took a course in Western literature. Part of the book of Job was in the textbook. He had heard that religion was poison and that the Bible was no good. But he fell in love with Job and after much searching found an old Bible, most others having been burned. He read the Gospels and when the "Gang of Four" was imprisoned, he went to church, confessed Christ as Lord, was baptized, and went to study at Nanjing Theological Seminary. The grace of God is now blessing the fruit of the church's suffering. But it was the conversion of the church, the repentance of the church, that made it possible.

The church in the West, and particularly in the United States, has much to learn from the church in China. We can learn that we live by grace, not by our power, might, friendship with society, wealth, or even by our colleges or church buildings. The Chinese Christians told us repeatedly that only a Christ-centered and trinitarian faith was able to sustain them and give them confidence. The church in the West has not experienced much suffering, and God forbid that we must. Rather, we should learn from the experiences of the Chinese Christians. Namely, we must learn that a converted church that does not seek power and is not hungry for the accolades of the world, approval of the rich, or high visibility in television ratings will by its poverty and servanthood be a most powerful witness to the One of whom we read, "Foxes have holes, and birds of the air have nests; but the Son of man has nowhere to lay his head" (Matt. 8:20). Such a church will produce a committed faculty, committed students, and committed leaders that will by their very lives and thought again cut down the sacred oak of Wotan and claim the West for Christ.

Similarly, we must learn from the experiences of Russian Christians. I began by reporting on a meeting with an Orthodox deacon and his vision of his country being won to Christ. It is a bold vision but one rooted again in the experience and suffering of the church. From many like experiences in Russian churches, one senses the ideal of holiness and sanctification — two words, I suspect, not mentioned very much in the American church, whether of the left or right, moderate or inerrant, liberal or conservative. But in Eastern Europe the holy life of the believer is a primary form of evangelism. They are daily questioned: "Why don't you get drunk? Why do your families stay together? Why don't you steal?" In the American reaction to Puritanism and its legalistic attitude (e.g., "I don't smoke, I don't drink, and I don't go with those who do"), we lost the ethical imperative of biblical faith demanding that we "be holy, for I am holy" (Lev. 11:44). The result, unfortunately, is that the artificiality of much of American Christianity has contributed to the weakness of our colleges. A sanctified church is not a sanctimonious church, which we often confuse with each other. From our brothers and sisters in Russia, I believe we can learn that the holy life is a positive and affirming life that communicates in a very deep way the mystery and joy of Jesus Christ. If we learn that, we will have come a long way toward conversion of the church.

The question remains, "Can Christian higher education be a part of the conversion of the West?" The answer is yes, if Christian colleges regain the vision of the unity of all things in Jesus Christ as the universal center around whom and in whom all truth coheres. George Buttrick reminded his generation:

> The long debate about how Christian education should be centered — whether in the pupil, or teacher, or school, or curriculum, or church — reveals what inroads the secular mind has made, and shows the tepidness of our belief. The center and burning focus should be Christ, Son of man and Son of God, as in all great ages of Christian history.[29]

When Billy Graham was in the Soviet Union, he preached in a city where a Baptist pastor had many young secular friends. The pastor invited an architect to attend one of the services, and he came along with ten other friends. The pastor could tell that he was moved by Graham's call for conversion. There was no room to invite people to come forward, so Dr. Graham asked all those ready to follow Christ to raise their hands. The young architect looked around. None of his friends raised their hands, and he did not raise his either. Later his wife told how he drove home silently and did not speak. At home his wife began to cook supper. She called her husband when it was time to eat, but could not find him. She looked upstairs in the bedroom and downstairs in the living room. She called and could not find her husband, but then she passed the bathroom and heard sobbing inside. She opened the door,

---

29. George Buttrick, *Christ and Man's Dilemma* (Nashville: Abingdon-Cokesbury Press, 1946), pp. 150-51.

and there she saw her husband with his hand raised accepting Christ. With tears running down his face, he hugged his wife and said, "I found something tonight I've been looking for all my life. I've found that God loves me and accepts me in Jesus Christ."

Conversion is the call of Christ to every generation of men and women. It is a call to the Christian college to teach young people the mystery of God's grace beyond the truth of science — beyond cause and effect — to show that mystery revealed in Jesus Christ, in whom the final purpose of history shall be revealed. God give us the grace and courage to so teach and so live in order that our generation may be evangelized and won to Christ.

QUESTIONS FOR REFLECTION AND DISCUSSION

1. Lotz sees Christian higher education as an essential element in the re-conversion of the West, and argues that Christian colleges and universities should find their *raison d'être* in a missiological context. Is it, and do they? Why or why not?

2. In accounting for where we are and how we got here, Lotz appeals to Newbigin's claim that modern science pushed questions of value out of the picture, giving "fact" pride of place. He then turns to Visser 't Hooft in identifying issues for Christian higher education in a "neo-pagan society." What is the connection between the two? Would the Christian theology of creation, sex, and justice that Lotz advocates be an adequate response to the historical and intellectual forces generative of today's neo-pagan culture?

3. Lotz calls for repentance on the part of Christian scholars and the church-related institutions that they serve. Of what does he think repentance is needed? What would be the practical import of taking this counsel seriously?

4. What, precisely, does Lotz suggest can be learned from the experience of the church overseas, and how does it bear on the project of Christian higher education in America?

FURTHER RELATED WORK BY THIS AUTHOR

Lotz, Denton, ed. *Spring Has Returned: Listening to the Church in China.* McLean, Va.: Baptist World Alliance, 1987.

Chapter Nine

The Challenge of Radical Christianity for the Christian College

ANTHONY CAMPOLO

Tracing the historical development of Christian colleges is no easy task. There are so many of them, and each of them is so unique, that it becomes difficult to develop a typology or to make generalizations. Nevertheless, utilizing the approach of German sociologist Max Weber, I will endeavor to define the characteristics of three types of Christian colleges. In a Weberian sense, these types are pure types. They are hypothetical constructs, needed for the purposes of comparison and evaluation. Actual colleges will conform to one or another of these ideal types in varying degrees, and many of the schools will bear traits of each of the types. Of course I engage in this effort not as a mere academic enterprise, but in order to highlight a kind of Christian college education to which we should aspire. This now largely lost ideal is what I call the radical Christian college. Radical Christian colleges are characterized by a counterculturalism and social engagement that finds its ground in a rich and enriching commitment to biblical Christianity.

Campolo presented the H. I. Hester Lectures during the June 1980 meeting of the ASBCS. He adapted this chapter from the July-August 1980 issue of *The Southern Baptist Educator.*

ANTHONY CAMPOLO

Three Types of Christian Colleges

The first group of colleges is composed of the *traditional denominationally sponsored* colleges. These schools were founded before our nation declared its independence from England, and schools of this type have continued to be created through the years. In the earliest days, they were primarily created to train church leadership for the New World. Schools like Harvard, Yale, Princeton, and Brown were founded by Christian groups to train pastors for the settlers in the New World and for their children. Schools like Dartmouth and Williams aimed at fulfilling a missionary calling by training a generation of young men to evangelize the Native Americans and peoples around the world. These schools also served to fulfill the cultural mandate of Christianity as understood by John Calvin and others in the Reformed tradition. The Protestant theologians contended that all knowledge reflected the glory of God, and that learning enhanced appreciation of God and resulted in more intelligent worship. All truth pointed to God, and the exploration of truth was believed to be a means of bringing humanity into a closer relationship with the Almighty.

Further, as sociologist Robert Merton perceived, the labors of these early academicians were the result of imperatives suggested by the Protestant Work Ethic. According to Merton, Protestant scholars believed that it was their God-given calling to expand all fields of knowledge through research and logic. However, there were ironic consequences to their efforts. While Christianity motivated them to make great discoveries in science and philosophy, their findings led them to question the very faith from which their efforts had emanated. In short, the Protestant Work Ethic motivated scholars to make discoveries that led them to doubt their theological belief systems.[1] Following Merton's train of thinking, it should be no surprise to discover that gradually these Christian colleges were rationalized into secular institutions. Mainstream denominations created new institutions to fulfill the purposes abandoned by these early schools. Unfortunately, these later creations all too often followed the pattern into secularization of their predecessors.

At the turn of the last century a new group of Christian colleges that

---

1. Robert K. Merton, "The Puritan Spur to Science," in *The Sociology of Science: Theoretical and Empirical Investigations* (Chicago: University of Chicago Press, 1973), pp. 228-53.

represented a second type came into being. I call them *sectarian colleges.* They were created to resist liberal theological tendencies that were becoming evident in America as a result of new European thought. The higher and lower criticisms of the Scripture emerging from German scholarship seemed to be a serious challenge to the authority of Scripture. Neo-Hegelian philosophy had been reinterpreted in theological terms and introduced to the American academic community in varying forms of process theology. But the challenge that seemed most serious to traditional Christianity was the one posed by the doctrine of biological evolution.

It is perhaps hard for us to imagine the fearful reactions to Darwinian thought then evident among Christians of all stripes and persuasions. Norman Furniss, one of the prime commentators on the fundamentalist controversy, perceives evolution as the primary issue dividing Christianity into fundamentalist and liberal camps.[2] In this controversial context, sectarian colleges were created to provide a Christian education for young people without allowing them to be subverted by "un-Christian" doctrines and to free them from the secularizing tendencies that were inherent in the general culture. Church people had seen too many of their children lose their faith in the context of the liberal institutions of learning where they had gone for college educations. Many of them looked for schools that would protect their children, educate them, and return them home still committed to the Christian faith with which they were reared.

These schools are noteworthy for their doctrinal statements in which they clearly delineate a strong commitment to the authority of Scripture, to the belief in miracles, to the virgin birth, and to the visible second coming of Christ. These schools also put a strong emphasis on the integration of faith and knowledge. However, the ideas and findings of the arts and sciences that could not be reconciled to their *a priori* theological belief systems were quickly rejected. Their doctrinal statements were touchstones used to test all knowledge. Any information that could not be harmoniously integrated into their *a priori* theologies was deemed illegitimate. There was little attempt to modify theology in light of new scholarship or scientific discoveries. Knowledge contrary to the accepted

2. Norman F. Furniss, *The Fundamentalist Controversy, 1918-1931* (New Haven: Yale University Press, 1954).

understanding of Scripture was looked upon as a part of a demonic plot to subvert Christianity and destroy the faith of God's people.

It is all too easy to judge harshly these sectarian fundamentalist institutions. In reality, they served a very necessary function. They kept the faith at a time when many Christians and Christian institutions reeled under the impact of new intellectual trends that were difficult to assimilate without producing secularization. These schools continued to turn out faithful servants of the gospel while the rest of American Christianity retrenched itself, evaluated the intellectual challenges posed by the new science and biblical scholarship, and developed a theology that could function in the new cultural climate. These institutions produced a disproportionate number of missionaries, evangelists, pastors, and denominational leaders. Many of the most prominent church leaders of our time openly acknowledge the debt that they have to the inspiration, guidance, and biblical knowledge that they gained at schools of this kind.

Beyond these two types, however, a third type bears attention: *radical Christian colleges.* These institutions grew out of the pre–Civil War revivals, led by such men as Charles Finney. Those who created these schools saw them as training centers for those who would be the agents that God would use to change his world. The founders of these schools were cognizant of the evils inherent in the social system, and believed that it was imperative to raise up a generation of young people who understood their world and knew how to change it into the kind of world that God willed it to be. They were particularly committed to the abolitionist movement, and believed that if the nation were to be purged from the ugly institution of slavery, it would require an array of intelligent, committed, and trained leaders. Using the typology of H. Richard Niebuhr, I would say that these schools were designed to produce "transformers of culture."

Out of this movement came such schools as Oberlin College, Antioch College, and Wheaton College. Many who now view Wheaton as a conservative institution do not realize that its founder, Jonathan Blanchard, was a committed abolitionist with ties to Oberlin and Knox Colleges who hoped to give birth to still another school that would produce radical social reformers. Oberlin provides an early model for this type of Christian college. It was modeled in accord with the New Testament community, rather than the contemporary business corporation. Whereas a structural analysis of contemporary colleges would view the trustees as the owners of the school, the administration and faculty as employees, and the students as patrons, the Oberlin model brought trustees, students, and faculty together as brothers and sisters in Christ. The school operated as an economic community. Faculty members were paid in accord with their needs, and students paid tuition in accord with their ability. All members of the academic community functioned as co-laborers in the causes to which they were committed. There was intimate sharing and social interaction among trustees, faculty, administration, and students. They endeavored to bear one another's burdens and tried to strengthen each other in the faith. The social and political issues that abounded in the society were discussed and evaluated in the midst of the constant interaction that occurred between all sectors of the Oberlin family. This kind of school was a rare event. Though many have sought to duplicate it, its like has not appeared often or for long.

Having provided some historical background for the origins of these three types of colleges, I will consider now the present status of each. The traditional denominationally sponsored schools have become secularized to various degrees. Most of them have cut their denominational ties. Bucknell University and Brown University are examples of this. Other denominational colleges have been able to maintain their commitments to Christian positions in spite of pressures to move them into nonreligious forms. Further, denominations such as the Reformed Church in America, the Missouri Synod Lutherans, the Christian Reformed Church, and the Mennonites have initiated new denominationally sponsored colleges. These schools, which gain the bulk of their financial support from denominational sources and recruit their students from the churches that sponsor them, have of necessity remained faithful to the purposes that gave them birth. These schools have served their denominations well and have provided their churches with qualified and dedicated leaders.

The graduates of these schools are imbued with American upper middle-class values. They fit easily into the leadership roles of existing institutions. They seldom challenge the structure of the existing social system. While they may carry some reformist values, they generally endorse the existing forms of the political and economic institutions. Once again using H. Richard Niebuhr's typology, I would have to consider these graduates as expressions of the Christ of Culture orientation. They believe that there are many ways in which the social system could be improved, but they basically believe in the ideology of American capitalism and the principles of a republican form of government. They are comfortable within the framework of American society and believe that if all citizens lived out the honesty and integrity prescribed by Scripture, America would be the kind of nation that God wills.

Sectarian colleges have not only survived, but have grown in recent years. They often attract those who reject denominational Christianity as being too liberal, and who are threatened by cultural tendencies. Bob Jones University, perhaps the most sectarian of the schools in this group, propagates, through radio and television, the view that most traditional denominational schools are worse than secular institutions because they attract Christian young people under the guise of being evangelical, when in reality they subvert the faith of those who attend.

Sociologists are quick to point out that one of the reasons these institutions grow is because of the homogeneous nature of their constituencies. Their students are all of the same socioeconomic and cultural background. They hold similar beliefs in politics and theology. Their concepts of personal morality are strikingly uniform. Indeed, sociological research shows that institutions with homogeneous traits grow the fastest. They project no ambiguities and relate well to specific constituencies. Contrary to most Christian colleges which give off mixed signals as to what they are and what they teach, these sectarian colleges leave no doubt as to what they are, what they believe, and who would be comfortable as part of their academic communities.

Regretfully, most sectarian colleges tend to endow themselves with what Robert Bellah would call "cultural religion." Their fundamentalist Christianity has become interwoven with conservative American politics. It is sometimes hard to differentiate the gospel from their right-wing political opinions. Opposition to such things as the Equal Rights Amendment, the union movement, the anti-war movement, disarmament, gay rights, and the pro-choice position on abortion have become hallmarks of their ideology. To say that they lack a social consciousness is to miss the point. These colleges are socially concerned, and their graduates are committed to effect change. The changes that they want to bring about would move the society to structures and lifestyles that belong to an earlier time, and to a manner of life that characterized America during those days when the nation was conditioned and controlled by a white Anglo-Saxon Protestant mentality. Perhaps the best example of this mixture of cultural religion and fundamentalist theology is expressed in Liberty University, under the direction of Jerry Falwell. In listening to the television programs that have been the basis of the growth and development of that school, one is hard put to differentiate Americanism from Christianity.

Radical Christian colleges have ceased to exist. Schools like Oberlin and Antioch have maintained a strong commitment to liberal social change, but they no longer legitimate their programs for social action solely on biblical grounds. Their actions are more informed by the broad principles of humanistic psychology. Wheaton College has tended to become more sectarian in its orientation, and is somewhat removed from the conceptualization of its founder. Radical Christian colleges committed to effecting biblically grounded social change — and thereby to enhancing human dignity, social justice, and economic freedom — simply do not exist, even though such colleges are needed. David Black, the president of Eastern University, is making a valiant effort to transform that school into an institution that reflects these commitments. He has made working for social justice an integral part of Eastern's mission statement. How far he can carry out his vision remains to be seen.

The Need for Radical Christian Colleges

Whatever its faults, significant though they may be, liberation theology has renewed attention to some central themes of Christianity. In particular, liberation theology reminds us that God acknowledges the poor and the oppressed in their struggles for justice and dignity. Associated with the rise of liberation theology, of course, are names like José Míguez Bonino, Gustavo Gutiérrez, and Camilo Torres. These Latin American writers have one thing in common — they are informed by a Marxian perspective. They see history as a class struggle between the haves and the have-nots, between the rich and the poor, between the oppressed and the oppressors, and in the midst of their own social situation, between the proletariat and the bourgeoisie. In this struggle, they believe that God does not remain neutral. They believe that Yahweh identifies with the poor and the oppressed in their struggle for social justice. They are convinced that God has identified with the proletarian segment of society as it struggles to establish dignity for people against what they believe to be a dehumanizing and oppressing situation between them and the bourgeoisie.

Liberation theologians look to Scripture for verification and legitimation. In the Old Testament they note that God chooses as his people not a powerful, wealthy group, but an oppressed people enslaved in Egypt. As these victims of political and economic oppression cry out for help in the midst of their misery, Yahweh hears their calls and champions their cause. In the Exodus story they observe a God who is allied with enslaved peoples against oppressors. When the people of Israel established themselves in the land of Canaan, they developed a stratification system similar to that which would exist in any society. Wealth became concentrated in the hands of an elite few, while a host of people suffered economic exploitation at the hands of this elite. Through his prophets, God speaks out against the rich and powerful who oppress the poor. For example, the book of Amos articulates God's identification with the lowest members of the socioeconomic order.

In the New Testament, this theme is continued. In the Magnificat, Mary announces that the purpose of the Savior would be to bring down the mighty from their seats of power and to lift up those who are of low degree. She proclaims that Emmanuel will feed the hungry and send away the rich empty. Jesus initiates his ministry by saying that he has come with good news for the poor, and warns that the rich and the powerful will find it more difficult to enter into his kingdom than it is for a camel to go through the eye of a needle. In parable after parable, he makes it clear that the judgment of Yahweh is against the rich who have lived without sensitivity to the sufferings of the poor. Perhaps no parable expresses this more clearly than the parable of the rich man and Lazarus.

On the American scene, theologians have picked up this radical theme. John Howard Yoder, a Mennonite scholar, famously makes it clear in *The Politics of Jesus* that Jesus came into the world to declare the Year of Jubilee. He contends that Jesus was calling for the redistribution of wealth and the creation of a new social order in which people would no longer rule from positions of power.[3] William Stringfellow, in *An Ethic for Christians and Other Aliens in a Strange Land,* calls upon his readers to view the contemporary political-economic system as the Babylon de-

3. John Howard Yoder, *The Politics of Jesus: Vicit Agnus Noster,* 2nd ed. (Grand Rapids: Eerdmans, 1994).

scribed in the Book of Revelation. He goes on to argue that this Babylon is condemned of God and must ultimately be brought down. He suggests that those who are allied with the values of the dominant socioeconomic order are the enemies of God and will suffer destruction when this system comes to an end.[4]

James Cone sets forth a radical position as well in his book, *A Black Theology of Liberation.* He calls upon white people to recognize that when Jesus was born he was born to an oppressed group of people. In the words of Cone, "Because God has made himself known in the history of oppressed Israel and decisively in the Oppressed One, who is Jesus Christ, it is impossible to say anything about him without seeing him as being involved in the contemporary liberation of all oppressed people."[5] Cone carries his message into the area of hermeneutics. He points out that any presentation of Scripture is an interpretation. Middle-class people will read into the Scriptures middle-class values, and impart to Scripture a middle-class understanding. Oppressed peoples will find in Scripture meanings and values that relate to their social condition. They will understand the Bible as the record of God's endeavor to lead the oppressed of the world into a condition of hope and dignity. It is easy to suggest that one interpretation might be as good as another, but Cone will not allow us to escape so easily. He argues that the interpretation provided by the oppressed is the central one, because the Bible was written by an oppressed people, for an oppressed people, about a Savior who identified with oppressed people.[6] Only by adopting the consciousness of the oppressed can one expect to grasp the meaning of Scripture and enter into the kingdom of heaven.

As a middle-class American, I would like to dismiss these radical theologians in a cavalier fashion by merely allowing that they have some "interesting" insights into Scripture. Unfortunately, I feel that there is a great deal of truth to their message. I believe that God has identified with the poor and the oppressed. I am coming to see that there is something incongruous about my life of affluence and my claim to be a follower of one who emptied himself of all wealth and became a suffering

4. William Stringfellow, *An Ethic for Christians and Other Aliens in a Strange Land* (Waco, Tex.: Word, 1973).

5. James H. Cone, *A Black Theology of Liberation* (Philadelphia: J. B. Lippincott, 1970), p. 116.

6. Cone, *A Black Theology of Liberation,* pp. 202-3.

servant. I am haunted by a Jesus who tells me that unless I deny myself, sell whatsoever I have, and give to the poor, I cannot be one of his disciples. Increasingly his message to the rich young ruler speaks to me, and I am coming to see that Christian discipleship requires a commitment to the poor and the oppressed, and a readiness to give up my position of wealth and power to follow a humble Galilean.

If Christian colleges are committed to train young people to be disciples for Christ in the world, can they ignore those things that are being said to us by these new and often shrill spokespersons for radical theology? If our schools are to be truly Christian, can they ignore the call to train up a generation of young people who will cast their lot with the downtrodden and use their knowledge and training to champion the cause of the oppressed? Might not the Christian college be called upon to inspire a generation of young people to live out a radical commitment to Christ, to endeavor to structure society so as to eliminate oppression, amend economic injustice, and encourage participatory democracy? Christian colleges today can hardly be considered hotbeds for the rearing of persons who would disturb the social order, in spite of the fact that they claim to be inspired by one who was accused of "stirring up the people."

Ultimately, I reject the Marxian basis of liberation theology. I differ with Bonino who sees the realization of Christian ideals as concomitant with the abolition of capitalism. I am a capitalist, and I believe that capitalism is an expression of democracy. With Michael Novak, I contend that freedom implies a free enterprise system, and I argue that when people are not free to express themselves in an economic fashion in accord with their wills, they are not free. Rather than destroying the political-economic structure that is capitalistic, I call for its restructuring in accord with biblical principles. I believe that it should be the task of Christian colleges to train a generation of young people to understand the way in which that system works, not accepting its consequences as inevitable, but changing the system into one that fulfills God's will in history.

Will Christian colleges train young people to understand how the social structure's present form facilitates unjust distribution of resources, oppression, and political inequality? Will the graduates of Christian colleges be equipped to make those changes in the social structure that are a prerequisite to the fulfillment of God's will? Will they know how to invade the institutions of society for the purpose of transforming them into what they ought to be? It is to such ends that a Christian college should be committed. What would be the character of such a college? Needless to say, my answer will be more of a vision than a pragmatic model. Nonetheless, insofar as it is possible I shall try to outline a proposed curriculum and social structure for such an institution.

The Nature of Radical Christian Colleges

A Christian college that takes seriously the insights of radical Christianity would sensitize its faculty to teach from a new perspective and develop courses to answer new questions. The new curriculum would be organized around the religion department, and biblical scholars would have the task of fostering dialogue in each of the academic disciplines of the institution to the end that each discipline might be made aware of the biblical imperatives that are central to its course of study. Theology would once again be the queen of the sciences, informing all other disciplines as to what should be the focus of their respective concerns. The faculty of the religion department would have to have a basic understanding of the content and discussions that are presently a part of each area of study. In order to accomplish this, it would be essential for the professors of religion to be sitting in on courses offered in the institution. One year they might study sociology and another political science and in still another economics. Only by involved study in each of the academic fields of the institution could the religion faculty gain the understanding that would be prerequisite to relating biblical material to all fields of knowledge.

The religion department would have to conduct ongoing seminars for the rest of the college faculty, to inform them of insights derived from biblical scholarship and theological reflection. In such seminars the faculty would have the opportunity to provide feedback, insights, and perspectives on theology that could only come from the perspectives of their respective areas of knowledge. The religion faculty would be responsible for an ongoing educational process in which the entire faculty would become involved in a process aimed at spelling out the implications of biblical revelation for each of the academic disciplines. Every effort would be made to explore God's purposes in history, and each academic program would be understood in terms of how it contributes to the creation of God's kingdom. In short, the religion department would primarily lead an educational process for the rest of the faculty. Its main task would be to sensitize colleagues to the ways in which Scripture speaks to every area of human endeavor. The teaching of students in traditional religion courses would only be their secondary responsibility. The students would not be neglected spiritually in such a plan. Instead of religion being a separate course in the curriculum, biblical truth would be interwoven with all academic material so that theological insight would be a part of what was learned in every course of study.

It is hard to speculate as to how the actual content of courses would change under the impact of such a process, but it is important to make some cursory suggestions on the form of such courses in order to clarify what is meant by a radical Christian college. First of all, the business and economics department would be strikingly different from those departments as they presently exist in Christian schools. (My visits to Christian colleges have led me to believe that there is presently little to differentiate their programs from business and economics as offered in secular institutions.) Scholars like E. F. Schumacher would be given serious consideration.[7] The program would evaluate economic models for Third World countries that are based on what he calls "appropriate" or "intermediate" technology. Students would learn how to upgrade economic productivity in poor nations without employing massive technology with its concomitant disruptions of village life. Efforts would be made to develop an economic substructure for emerging nations that would be aimed at meeting the needs of the general population, rather than maximizing profits for a limited number of stockholders.

At Eastern College we have worked with some students along such lines. In conjunction with the Ball Corporation of Muncie, Indiana, a food cannery has been designed that can be purchased and made operational for less than $25,000. Three of my students put such a cannery into operation in the nation of Niger. They have taught the indigenous people how to run this cannery. Since the technology involved was at a very low level, it required less than a year for the people of Niger to become totally capable of running the cannery themselves. Students

7. Ernst Friedrich Schumacher, *Small Is Beautiful: Economics as if People Mattered* (New York: Harper and Row, 1973).

taught them the techniques of bookkeeping, management, and technical maintenance. Because of the low cost of the cannery, it has become possible for a group of Nigerois to purchase the cannery and run it as a community cooperative. The cannery is designed to increase the profit margin of the small farmers in the area who hitherto had experienced significant loss of their crops at harvest time. Prior to the operation of the cannery, there had been an inadequate infrastructure for the preserving and transporting of food to the population centers of Niger, so that these farmers had been incapable of marketing their crops at harvest time without a significant proportion undergoing spoilage. The cannery offers to the small farmers of the region the possibility that none of their crops will be lost, and that all they produce will be saleable. What is more, the availability of food will be increased dramatically without increasing the amount that is actually grown. Food will be abundantly available on a year-round basis, rather than only at harvest time. In addition to all of these positive social services, the cannery will reap a profit for those who are involved in its development, maintenance, and operation.

This is the kind of economic development that needs to be studied and implemented in poor nations. Cottage industries, upgrading of small farming units, cooperative buying programs, and other business projects must be studied and tried in order to discover effective means for eliminating poverty in poor nations of the world. It is possible to upgrade dramatically the economic well-being of Third World countries without introducing the disruptions of industrial urbanization that have been all too prevalent in the models hitherto employed. We have witnessed the migrations of Third World populations to their respective capital cities, with the consequence that those cities have been characterized by massive unemployment, dehumanization, collapse of moral systems, and a breakdown of family life. It is imperative to develop models for economic growth that will allow people to remain in their villages and continue life in accord with their traditional cultures.

Students in business and economics would be trained to evaluate the practices of multinational corporations. Conglomerates such as Gulf & Western and Alcoa have vast resources in capital and technical skills. These corporate structures need not be driven out of Third World nations. Instead, the Christian college should train a generation of business leaders who are capable of leading these corporations into investment

151

policies and production schemes that will meet the needs of the nations in which they function.

Moreover, while we may commit ourselves to social development via capitalism, we must not allow unqualified forms of capitalistic philosophy to go unchallenged. The primary purpose of production should not be the creation of profits, but rather meeting the needs of people. Industrial economies can often make great profits by designing products that meet artificially created wants rather than genuine human needs. Industrial economies are prone to waste, and even may require waste in order to survive. Capitalism may need qualification so that an economy emerges which, together with the technologies it generates, "has a human face."[8]

The political science departments of radical Christian colleges would do more than just analyze the ways in which political processes function. They would be sensitive to the dictum, "Philosophers describe history, but the real task is to change it." The students would study the political mechanisms that are essential for the creation of world peace. They would seek to understand the military-industrial complex that has too often stimulated the nations of the world into ominous arms races. They would endeavor to understand how to gain and use political power in accord with biblical values.

In 1974, I decided to enter the race for the U.S. Congress in the Fifth District of Pennsylvania as an anti-war candidate. I was opposed to what was happening in Southeast Asia, but I did not see the answer in the destruction of the American political system. I believed that the American political process could be made to work for peace and justice. Over a hundred of my students at Eastern College became actively involved in that campaign. They attended precinct meetings and state political caucuses, and became part of platform committees. They went door-to-door sharing their ideas and convictions. None of them became cynical in spite of the fact that the election was lost. We won the primary, did respectably in the general election, and the students became convinced that the American political process was a viable instrument for facilitating the kinds of changes that they believed to be ordained of God.

Leaders with a keen understanding of political and economic organization will be absolutely necessary if the American economy is to be

8. Schumacher, *Small Is Beautiful,* pp. 138-51.

redesigned into a less wasteful system. If we cut down on the number of automobiles and televisions produced; if we diminish consumption of cigarettes, alcohol, and sugar; and if we buy less meat, there will be a need to relocate those who are presently involved in producing these things. There is no question that the political-economic structure must be redesigned; the question that remains is whether or not the new design will incarnate Christian values. In the future, Americans will either be dragged screaming into a lifestyle and social order that is simpler, less wasteful, and more responsible, or they will be led into such a future by responsible Christian leaders. Will Christian colleges produce these leaders?

The biology department would be called upon to apply its knowledge to the problems of producing optimum crops with maximum nutrition. The students in this field would learn the lessons of ecologists, and guide the Christian community to live responsibly in relationship to the environment. With biblical insight, they would be able to show that it is sin to pollute the atmosphere and the rivers of the planet. They would help us all to see that God's commandment to rule over nature requires ecological responsibility.

The social sciences would make important contributions to the education of students in this new college. Committed to a volitional understanding of human personality, the psychology department would promote a view that sees us as responsible for our actions and capable of change. Advocating a social action framework of thought, they would abandon any behavioral model that would diminish the dignity and freedom of persons. They would help us to understand the processes that generate altruism and sacrifice in the human personality and show us the way to create the psychic wholeness that is responsible to others and to God. Such a course of study would show the weaknesses in that brand of humanistic psychology that has created what Tom Wolfe has called the "me decade"[9] and what Christopher Lasch called "the culture of narcissism."[10]

The sociology department would have to escape from the value-free orientation suggested by one of its founders, Max Weber. Like Auguste

9. Wolfe works his satiric wit on the "me decade" in *The Bonfire of the Vanities* (New York: Farrar, Straus and Giroux, 1987).

10. Christopher Lasch, *The Culture of Narcissism: American Life in an Age of Diminishing Expectations,* rev. ed. (New York: W. W. Norton, 1991).

Comte, Emile Durkheim, and Henri de Saint-Simon, those teaching sociology would need to understand society in order that they might know those aspects of the social system that hurt human development and be able to promote those social forces that make for healthy social equilibrium. The oppressive nature of racism would be explored so that by understanding it, we would have some help in learning how to destroy it; the social conditions that foster sexism would be studied so that they could be counteracted; and ways would be found to maintain a stratification system without oppression.

Efforts to eliminate destructive ethnocentrism would be guided by the anthropology department, whose faculty would not maintain an ethically neutral position, as is inherent in the relativistic structural functionalism that informs most contemporary anthropological study. Alternate models, such as that provided by Teilhard de Chardin, would be tested to see if they offered help in understanding cultural development toward the kind of social wholeness prescribed by Jesus. Students in business, politics, and world missions would not be allowed to go from this college to work in Third World nations without a grasp of ethnomethodology and cross-cultural appreciation.

The role of the arts would in no way be minimized. Literature, music, and art would not be reduced to the didactic function that they often have in Christian institutions. The arts would be used as instruments of humanization that lift the human spirit to its most aesthetic forms of expression. Herbert Marcuse points out that great art does not so much describe what is, as it makes us sensitive to what is not. Art stimulates dissatisfaction with the limitations of our experiences, and stimulates an appetite for dimensions of existence that have been excluded by the one-dimensionality of our contemporary culture. Art becomes the ultimate agent of revolution, and it is for this reason that true art has always been suppressed by totalitarian regimes. Tyrants want to maintain power by maintaining the illusion that the systems they perpetuate supply all human needs. True art breaks through the propaganda and stimulates the consciousness of what has been lost. Art gives expression to the groanings that cannot be uttered, and reminds the people of any society of what is not yet and ought to be.

In a radical Christian college, extracurricular activities would have to be reevaluated. The joy of athletics would not be ignored, but the question of scholarships would have to be reviewed. In this Christian college, students would receive financial aid in accord with their needs unrelated to whether or not they could play ball. Competitive athletics would not be ignored. However, students would not be recruited merely on the basis of athletic prowess, but on the basis of commitment to the cause of Christ. I need not press the growing tragedy of the athletic emphasis that has become a part of many Christian schools.

Chapel would be a focal point for campus life. It would be in the chapel services that the emerging ideology of the school would be articulated and consolidated. It would be there that the president, faculty, and students would share with one another what they are thinking and what they believe. The chapel services would be times of rejoicing, wherein the members of the academic community could tell of the great things that they see God doing to bring about the fullness of his kingdom.

Undoubtedly, you have detected that there would be an array of extracurricular activities related to the courses of the college. Students would learn about politics through involvement. Models for economic development would be tested in real-life situations. Social service programs would be implemented in actual practice. The students in business administration would be required to spend time working in association with corporate executives so as to gain firsthand knowledge of problems and possibilities in such positions.

The organizational structure for the radical Christian college might take a page from the history of Oberlin College and seek to create a community that would bring together the trustees, administration, faculty, and students. Every effort would be made to make all the persons related to the institution loving brothers and sisters in Christ. The trustees would have to be more than once-a-year visitors. They would have to be in constant contact and dialogue with administration, faculty, and students. They would have to understand the tensions of campus life and be able to share their visions with all the members of the academic community.

Teachers would have to see themselves as more than pure academicians. They could not be like those college teachers, too evident on many campuses, who teach their courses and then leave. They would have to be faculty members who seek *koinonia* rather than academic status. They would be paid in accord with their need rather than their rank, and their commitment to the school would be out of loyalty to the body of Christ.

The aim of this institution would be to produce graduates who do not fit into the social system comfortably, but who are lovingly dissatisfied with their world, who will be committed to nonviolent social change, and who know how to make such change a reality. They will have worked hard to define the kind of society they want to create and will be constantly evaluating their model against the requisites of Scripture.

Many of these graduates will go into church vocations. Some may find themselves in the pastorates of traditional churches communicating their vision and their hopes for the future to congregations that I believe are waiting for this message. Others may experiment with new forms of church life, developing congregations that do not own buildings because their resources are committed to meeting human needs. Many will experiment with being unpaid clergy, adopting the model of the worker-priest of France, endeavoring to carry the gospel into the marketplace while bringing the world of the marketplace into the circle of the church.

All of this may be characterized as an unrealistic dream, or an impractical vision, yet we must be reminded of the Scripture which teaches us that when the young men no longer dream dreams and the old men lose their vision the people perish. We all sense that there is something radically wrong with the world, and perhaps it remains for us to establish a radical Christian college that will create the leaders who will lead us into a radically different tomorrow.

QUESTIONS FOR REFLECTION AND DISCUSSION

1. What features of Campolo's three types of Christian college (traditional denominationally sponsored, sectarian, and radical Christian colleges) best describe the character of your institution?

2. Campolo rejects the Marxian perspectives that undergird some versions of liberation theology, but accepts their reminder of the biblical message that God cares for the poor, downtrodden, and oppressed. On his view, Christian colleges cannot in good faith ignore Scripture's call to social justice. Do you share his view that Christian colleges ought to inspire their students to "eliminate oppression, amend economic injustice, and encourage participatory democracy"? Why or why not?

3. On Campolo's account, radical Christian colleges "have ceased to exist," for "Christian colleges today can hardly be considered hotbeds for the rearing of persons who would disturb the social order." What explanations are there for the demise of radical Christian colleges? Are the difficulties that would-be radical Christian colleges encounter surmountable?
4. What, if anything, do you find compelling about Campolo's "impractical vision" of a radical Christian college? What amendments or qualifications would you add?

FURTHER RELATED WORK BY THIS AUTHOR

Campolo, Anthony. *Wake Up America! Answering God's Radical Call While Living in the Real World.* San Francisco: HarperSanFrancisco, 1991.

———. *Can Mainline Denominations Make a Comeback?* Valley Forge, Pa.: Judson Press, 1995.

———. *Revolution and Renewal: How Churches Are Saving Our Cities.* Louisville: Westminster/John Knox Press, 2000.

Chapter Ten

Christian Higher Education in the Twenty-First Century and the Clash of Civilizations

DENTON LOTZ

Interest in Samuel P. Huntington's *The Clash of Civilizations and the Re-making of the World Order,* much discussed since its publication in 1996, has only intensified following the September 11, 2001, terrorist attacks in New York and Washington, D.C. Some have called the book, with some exaggeration, prophetic. Unquestionably, it is a challenging and seminal book, one that helps us to understand the new world in which we are living since the fall of communism. Educators concerned about gaining deeper understanding of our complex world politically, socially, culturally, and certainly religiously will find this book instructive. Huntington's work provides insights that, at least indirectly, speak to the continued relevance of Christian higher education. Indeed, precisely because the twenty-first century may witness growing friction among civilizations, Christian liberal arts education is more important now than ever.

To this end, several central claims made by Huntington should be explored with sensitivity to the religious implications of his insights. This will be by way of setting up the challenges posed to Christian higher education by a multicivilizational world. I will then identify some theological resources to which Christian faculty might turn in respond-

---

Material in this chapter was presented as the H. I. Hester Lecture Series at the 1997 meeting of the ASBCS, and adapted for this collection from the Spring and Summer 1998 issues of *The Southern Baptist Educator.*

ing with integrity to these challenges. Finally, I will offer some practical imperatives that seem to follow given our context and our convictions. First, then, what of Huntington's "clash of civilizations"?

The Clash of Civilizations

In 1959 while an exchange student at Göttingen University in Germany I saw a little advertisement for a tour to the U.S.S.R. With enthusiasm we were able to round up about eleven other students to go with us. We had made ads in the student paper to recruit students for the trip and called the tour "Göttingen University Tour." I quickly learned that we were in the Cold War when I received a letter that the rector of the university wanted to see me. With great kindness the rector told me that I could not call the tour a "Göttingen University Tour" because he had not authorized it. Furthermore, he observed that West Germany and the U.S.S.R. were not on friendly terms and that this tour might be misinterpreted by people in the West.

However, the American students were enthusiastic and decided to go. Thus we began the long train ride to the U.S.S.R. via Helsinki, Finland. In Helsinki we boarded a train for Leningrad. This train took us to the border, and then we had to change at the last Finnish station to a Soviet train. The situation soon became somber for us. A Soviet soldier guarded the last wagon. The conductor looked us over suspiciously as we rolled out of the station into the U.S.S.R., and our passports and visas were checked carefully.

It was a long, twelve-hour train ride and we slept in comfortable bunk beds. Early in the morning we were awakened with "Tchai," tea. Suddenly we were in Leningrad, the hero city. Our communist guides took us to see the monument commemorating the long siege against the Nazis, nine hundred days and nine hundred nights. Thousands had been killed by the German fascists, and thousands had starved to death. There was no forgiveness — death was too near to the people to forget. We visited the famous Kazan Cathedral, which had become an anti-religious museum. There we saw the history of all that was bad about religion and Christianity. One was overwhelmed by the demonic impression of the Soviet state. It seemed like it would last forever. Atheism was a religion for the future. The Young Pioneers with their red scarves who guarded the heroes' tombs with rifles, and the little girls carrying flowers, seemed very romantic and heroic. The students at the university, fed with communist propaganda for years, were convinced that communism would win the world. The same experience was true in Moscow.

What a welcome relief it was to sit in the balcony of Central Baptist Church and hear the choir sing, "His eye is on the sparrow, and I know He watches me." The prayers, the hymns, the deep spirituality of these people who stood for hours . . . these memories will last forever. And then back into the bitter cold, past Lenin and Stalin's tomb, the reverence and the awe. What was the future of the church? Little did I realize, and little did they realize, that one day in 1989 the Berlin Wall would come tumbling down and the whole communist system with it.

For almost fifty years the world was divided into two camps: the capitalists and the communists, or perhaps as we liked to think, between those who loved freedom and those who suffered from a lack of it. The Cold War was the force that dictated all of our foreign policy, our economy, and our military. Anti-communism or anti-imperialism was the slogan of the day. Can it only be so few years since we lived in that world? Children were brought up in fear of the Bomb. Peace conferences were held. Helsinki Accords were made. The world seemed tottering on the verge of extinction by a nuclear war. Then one day the walls suddenly fell, and we are still trying to figure out where we have been and where we are going.

Professor Huntington's book is an outstanding road map to help us interpret the new situation in which the world now finds itself. His main theme is that "culture and cultural identities, which at the broadest level are civilizational identities, are shaping the patterns of cohesion, disintegration, and conflict in the post–Cold War world."[1] In other words, no longer is the conflict one of an overarching conflict of communism versus capitalism, long symbolized in the demonizing language that characterized the U.S.S.R. as "the evil empire" and the U.S. as leader of the "decadent and imperialist West."

On Huntington's account, future conflicts or "clashes" in the twenty-first century will be civilizational, and thus to a certain extent religious, since religion is such a significant ingredient of what makes a culture a cul-

---

1. Samuel P. Huntington, *The Clash of Civilizations and the Remaking of World Order* (New York: Simon and Schuster), p. 20.

ture and a civilization a civilization. Until September 11, this fact was largely lost in much of modern academia because of its attempt to be politically correct and multicultural. And not just in academia was this true. Were the occasion not so stunningly grim, the media scramble to find "experts" able to speak competently to the religious dimensions of the terrorist attacks would have been laughable. One would hope that neither the academy nor the media will neglect serious attention to the religious character of life as in the past. Huntington, at least, gives good reasons not to do so, for his general point about the "civilizational" nature of twenty-first-century clashes is well supported through five lesser theses.

Multipolar and Multicivilizational Global Politics

Huntington claims, "For the first time in history, global politics is both multipolar *and* multicivilizational."[2] It was the Western hope that by modernizing the world we would Westernize the world. But in fact the opposite is true. Modernization has not produced a universal civilization, and non-Western societies have not become Western. In fact, though every empire has endeavored to unite the world — from Alexander the Great through the Greek and Roman empires, to the more modern British Empire and recent Soviet and American attempts — all these attempts have failed. Diversity, and of a deep-down rather than a superficial variety, is here to stay. Perhaps Rudyard Kipling was more prophetic than he realized when he said, "East is East, and West is West, and never the twain shall meet/Till earth and sky stand presently at God's great judgment seat."[3] Why is this? What issues are at stake?

Civilization, Huntington says, is "the highest cultural grouping of people and the broadest level of cultural identity people have short of that which distinguishes humans from other species. It is defined both by common objective elements, such as language, history, religion, customs, institutions, and by the self-identification of people."[4] What are the various civilizations that make up this new world order? Huntington lists seven, or possibly eight. They include Sinic (or Chinese), Japanese,

2. Huntington, *The Clash of Civilizations,* p. 21.
3. Rudyard Kipling, "The Ballad of East and West," in *Barrack-Room Ballads,* 2nd ed. (New York: Macmillan, 1898), p. 3.
4. Huntington, *The Clash of Civilizations,* p. 43.

Hindu, Islamic, Western, Orthodox Russian (Byzantine), Latin Ameri-can, and African (possibly). Significantly, he regards religion as the "cen-tral defining characteristic" of these various civilizations.[5] He notes, with Christopher Dawson, that the "great religions are the foundations on which the great civilizations rest."[6] If this is the case, modern education, particularly from elementary school to high school, is woefully inade-quate to meet the challenge of preparing citizens for the next century, since religion is almost totally excluded.

While typologies are helpful instruments to interpret broad and dif-ficult subjects, they always have their limits. Of Huntington's eight civi-lizations, four are largely Christian, even though they in some sense may be competing civilizations. Thus, to a certain extent his typology breaks down, for we are dealing with differences giving rise to far less than a conflict of "all against all."

Nonetheless, his main proposition that the world in which we live is a multicivilizational place holds fast, and recognizing this is basic to help us understand the present world clashes. Pick up a newspaper any day and you immediately see the problem. Whether it is Iranian students demon-strating against the German court's decision accusing its leaders of terror-ism, or the Pope telling European leaders that a united continent cannot ignore its Christian roots, or India and Pakistan threatening one another over Kashmir, or Russia fretting over the extension of NATO, or support of Serbia, or the "war on terrorism," the problem remains. The fact is that we live in a world of civilizational conflicts, which is shocking following the short-lived hope of "a new world order" after the fall of the Berlin Wall. Ethnocentric conflict is the order of the day whether between Bosnia and Serbia, Chechnya and Russia, Israel and Palestine, or the large con-flicts between China and the United States or Turkey and Greece.

What makes Huntington so interesting is that he evidently has a better grasp of the obvious characteristics of the world in which we live than many others in the mainstream academy. Ask the average teacher or professor to describe the most important characteristic of Western civili-zation and one would probably hear the words, democracy, freedom, technology, individualism, human rights, and so on, with little mention

5. Huntington, *The Clash of Civilizations,* p. 47.
6. Christopher Dawson, *Dynamics of World History* (LaSalle, Ill.: Sherwood Sugden Co., 1978), p. 128; quoted in Huntington.

of religion. Yet Huntington contends, "Western Christianity . . . is historically the single most important characteristic of Western civilization."[7] If this is true, what then does it bode for the present state of education in our lower schools and for higher education?

The Decline of Western Influence

Huntington also observes that "The balance of power among civilizations is shifting: the West is declining in relative influence; Asian civilizations are expanding their economic, military, and political strength; Islam is exploding demographically with destabilizing consequences . . . and non-Western civilizations are reaffirming the value of their own cultures."[8]

This theme is probably the most damning to the West and to the whole idea of Christianizing the world. The implication of this thesis is that after two hundred years of Christian missionary movement, the world is not inclined to become more Christian. If anything, there has been a reversion back to the great religions of the various cultures and civilizations. And what is the basis of this resurgence of religions, including Buddhism, Hinduism, and Islam? It is negatively "a reaction against secularism, moral relativism, and self-indulgence. . . ."[9] Interestingly enough, it is the young people who join the rising tide of Islamic fundamentalism. They have rejected the moderation of their parents. They are young, urban, and well educated. They have seen the decadence and double standards of the West. The overthrow of the Shah in Iran was largely a reaction to decadent Western culture. Not only Islamic fundamentalists, but well-educated Muslims, reject their Western education. Modernity or modern technology is not rejected, but "it is a rejection of the West and of the secular, relativistic, degenerate culture associated with the West."[10] Nowhere is this rejection seen more clearly than in the harsh rhetoric of radicals who rally on behalf of jihad against the West.

To a certain degree, evangelical Christians would agree with this analysis of Western culture. We have become so cowed by the media in speaking out against our own decadence, that we often fail to say what we ought

---

7. Huntington, *The Clash of Civilizations*, p. 70.
8. Huntington, *The Clash of Civilizations*, p. 20.
9. Huntington, *The Clash of Civilizations*, p. 98.
10. Huntington, *The Clash of Civilizations*, p. 101.

lest we be called radical right or fundamentalist. To succumb to such criticism, however, results in a loss of the prophetic ability to be a transforming power in our own society. And the need for transformation — for redemption through Christ — cannot be in doubt. The vulgarity of the modern media is an affront to the Christian hope for a redeemed humanity. The shock-rock group called Marilyn Manson features obscene lyrics on the occult, suicide, and torture in such songs as "Kiddie Grinder" and "Dried Up, Tied and Dead to the World." German television recently had a so-called comedy show that featured Christ nailing a dead goldfish to the cross and declaring, "So, in three days he will live again." Another program featured transsexuals dancing with an archbishop and yelling, "we forgive you, you dumb pig." It is no wonder that decent people in the Islamic world fearing this decadence would say, "Islam is the solution."

The revival of Hinduism in India, Buddhism in Japan, and indigenous religious practices among African nationals follows a similar pattern. In discovering their past, students become nationalistic and proud of their traditions. When I was a student in Germany I met a young Nigerian who came from a Christian background. He said, "I used to laugh at my father who worshiped sticks and stone. But no longer. When the whites in Berlin refused me a room because the lady was afraid her white sheets would become black from my skin, then I knew that something was wrong with Christianity. You fooled us. I am going back to my father's gods." What an indictment of the so-called Christian West!

The church needs to disassociate itself from the false view of Western civilization portrayed by secular humanism. Indeed, is it not the time for the church to be a counterculture against this decadence? Surely the case should be made that many great ideals and accomplishments of Western civilization are indebted to Christianity, the abandonment of which weakens values long cherished among us. Whence comes the great concern for personal freedom, human rights, care for the poor and downcast, and the search for justice? Are these not positive values that have shaped Western culture for centuries, and as a direct result of the Christian influence upon society? Recall Helmut Thielicke's words: "The freedom of the children of God is the great offense for every ideological tyranny."[11]

---

11. Helmut Thielicke, *The Freedom of the Christian Man: A Christian Confrontation with the Secular Gods,* trans. John W. Doberstein (New York: Harper and Row, 1963), p. 124.

Stability of Civilizational Identity

Huntington further holds that civilizations are recalcitrant to change. On his view, "A civilization-based world order is emerging: societies sharing cultural affinities cooperate with each other; efforts to shift societies from one civilization to another are unsuccessful; and countries group themselves around the lead or core states of their civilization."[12]

The fact is that people feel more comfortable with others who share the same values, language, culture, and religion. From personal relations to national relations, this holds true. Marriages of people of different religions usually are not well accepted by either family, making their life together difficult. This is true for nations also. Middle-Eastern culture is united by the Arabic language and Islam. Hinduism united India, and Buddhism Japan.

Military alliances, as well as economic, often develop along these civilizational fault lines. The eastward expansion of NATO shows the conflict between Western culture and Byzantine or Orthodox culture. Turkey finds itself in a very difficult situation. It is a secular Muslim state that wants to be part of the European Community, but until now it has been rejected, with many excuses, mainly about human rights being given. The Turkish leaders see it otherwise: "The real reason," said President Ozal in 1992, "is that we are Muslim, and they are Christian." The conflict continues to this day.

Huntington maintains that there are core states that must take the lead in holding together their civilizations. When the presence of a core state is lacking, there is often fighting within the civilization, as in the case of Western involvement in the Bosnian-Serbian conflict. Orthodoxy is led by Russia, and thus Russia became the guardian of Serbia, even against the wishes of Western Europe. Only when the United States entered the fray in Bosnia was Western power meaningfully exerted on the two other civilizational groups, and Orthodox and Muslim subsequently came together in the Dayton accords. Europe was not able to hold things together without the United States' core state status. This puts an enormous responsibility upon the core state, whichever one is in question, and this responsibility often gives rise to a struggle to maintain superior firepower, economic power, or political hegemony.

12. Huntington, *The Clash of Civilizations,* p. 20.

Likelihood of Civilizational Conflict

Unfortunately, the prospects for peace in the world of the twenty-first century are not great, for Huntington suggests that "The West's universalist pretensions increasingly bring it into conflict with other civilizations, most seriously with Islam and China; at the local level fault line wars, largely between Muslims and non-Muslims, generate 'kin-country rallying,' the threat of broader escalation, and hence efforts by core states to halt these wars."[13]

At this moment, United States forces are stationed in Korea and Japan, in Saudi Arabia and Afghanistan, in Europe, and off the coast of India. As the West's core state, the United States is basically in a position to interact, positively and negatively, with all the various civilizations. This means when conflict arises it is usually the United States that is forced to act as the world's policeman, and it is precisely this type of action that brings forth the wrath of other peoples and new nationalistic feelings.

To make matters worse, Huntington sees in such responses evidence of a new tribalism. In fact, on his view, "Civilizations are the ultimate human tribes, and the clash of civilizations is tribal conflict on a global scale."[14] Many Americans could not understand why the Islamic nations were so opposed to American involvement in defending Kuwait against the obviously tyrannical invasion of Saddam Hussein and Iraq in 1991. It is precisely because this may be, according to the distinguished Moroccan scholar, Mahdi Elmandjra, "la première guerre civilisationnelle" — the first civilizational war.[15] It was seen as a war against another Muslim country by a Christian nation. Thus, the prevailing attitude of Arabs was, "Saddam was wrong to invade, but the West was more wrong to intervene; hence Saddam is right to fight the West, and we are right to support him." No one knows the serious, long-term consequences of the current military and political intervention in Iraq, undertaken by President George W. Bush's so-called "coalition of the willing." Worldwide protests against the war, the fraying of relations between the United States and China, France, Germany, and Russia, and the apparent impotence of the United Nations to avert conflict all suggest the accuracy of

13. Huntington, *The Clash of Civilizations,* p. 20.
14. Huntington, *The Clash of Civilizations,* p. 205.
15. Cited in Huntington, *The Clash of Civilizations,* p. 246.

Huntington's claim about the likelihood of clashes in a multicivilizational world.

The Chastening of Western Arrogance

Not least of all, Huntington's account calls attention to the conditions under which the West will or will not flourish in the twenty-first century. He writes, "The survival of the West depends on Americans reaffirming their Western identity and Westerners accepting their civilization as unique not universal and uniting to renew and preserve it against challenges from non-Western societies. Avoidance of a global war of civilizations depends on world leaders accepting and cooperating to maintain the multicivilizational character of global politics."[16]

This sub-theme of Huntington is perhaps the most worrisome for concerned American Christians. It presents American Christians with a double-edged sword. On the one hand it says that whether we like it or not the United States is the core state that must defend Western identity. On the other hand it maintains that global war can only be avoided when we affirm the multicivilizational nature of the world. This poses a problem for the evangelical Christian. On the one hand, we need to re-Christianize or re-evangelize the West, and at the same time accept the *status quo* of the rest of the world. In other words, we need to accept the civilizational nature of the world.

What does this mean for Christian witness in non-Christian or non-Western societies? It is precisely these arguments of civilization that have been used against Western evangelism in Eastern Europe, and particularly Slavic Europe, since the end of communism. Former state churches have raised their flag as being "the" expression of Christianity, and all others are accused as sectarian and undermining of the unity of the country. For instance, on Easter Sunday morning in a small Romanian town the police stood by as a priest led about a thousand villagers in beating up a small congregation of nine Baptists who had come to worship in a rented apartment. Their clothes were torn from them, they were dragged and beaten, but were, providentially, able to escape with their lives. When they arrived in the next village and made known what had happened, complaining to the Metropolitan, they were met with the

---

16. Huntington, *The Clash of Civilizations,* pp. 20-21.

scornful words of the church leader: "That is the way peasants react. If you kick our souls, we will kick your bodies."

At the same time the West was defending Kuwait from Iraqi aggression, the Islamic government of Saudi Arabia refused the importation of Bibles to our troops in Desert Storm. How can we affirm the multicivilizational nature of the world (and I believe we must), and yet at the same time defend religious freedom and human rights for all? This will be the crucial question for the next century.

What is more difficult is how to re-evangelize the West. The Pope has called for the re-evangelization of Europe. His call made Lutheran and Reformed Church leaders in Europe very nervous. They worried about the re-Catholicization of Europe. And yet when one realizes that in Germany alone 500,000 leave the state church every year, something has to be done. When only 27 percent of East Germans believe in God, when a new paganism has come to France, Scandinavia, and Britain, what must be done? It has been said that there are more Muslims in the mosques on Friday in Britain than Anglicans in church on Sunday.

In the United States, among the greatest obstacles to evangelization are the intellectuals and the universities, many of which began as Christian institutions. While we want to acknowledge other civilizations, trends toward political correctness and multiculturalism have become a threat to the survival of the Western civilization. Huntington makes this serious observation about the multicultural intellectuals and publicists: "In the name of multiculturalism they have attacked the identification of the United States with Western civilization, denied the existence of a common American culture, and promoted racial, ethnic and other subnational cultural identities and groupings."[17] Even Arthur Schlesinger sounds the same warning, accusing these of seeing little other than crimes in Western heritage. Furthermore, he asserts, their "mood is one of divesting Americans of the sinful European inheritance and seeking redemptive infusions from non-Western cultures."[18]

Huntington concludes that if we are going to have peace, and avoid a clash of civilizations that only produces wars, then there must be "understanding and cooperation among the political, spiritual, and intellec-

17. Huntington, *The Clash of Civilizations,* p. 305.
18. Arthur M. Schlesinger, Jr., *The Disuniting of America: Reflections on a Multicultural Society* (New York: W. W. Norton, 1992), pp. 66-67, 123; cited in Huntington.

tual leaders of the world's major civilizations."[19] Is this possible? Do Christians have anything to contribute to securing such understanding and cooperation?

Christian Theological Contributions within a Multicivilizational World

I have expended some effort in describing these aspects of Huntington's work because they bear critically upon the nature and mission of Christian higher education in the twenty-first century. Of course Huntington's work is not a theological tract, and thus avoids theological answers even if it is a shrewd observation of the present crisis. What will be the Christian response to the picture he paints? Paul Tillich once observed that secular culture pushes the church to irrelevance, and that the two ways the church has responded — radical rejection of and radical adaptation to culture — have been failures. Those on the right who want to preserve the Christian West may see the answer in establishing a Christian and righteous nation by force of law, by legislation, and by control of the ballot or the government. Those on the left who want to preserve the West by adapting would ultimately give up to a religionless Christianity. Indeed, this is precisely the situation in which we find ourselves today, not only politically, but also educationally. By identifying everything as broadly Christian, many former denominational schools have given up their Christian heritage completely and their new religion has become multiculturalism. The other side has too often become sectarian and arrogant, alienating the very people they need to re-evangelize and Christianize in the West.

A better way must be found, and reflection upon Christian theological resources within the context of church-related higher education can help. Indeed, Christians have a principled basis for appreciatively acknowledging the diversity that is part and parcel of a multicivilizational world, yet doing so all the while professing abiding commitment to the "great things" of the gospel. Why is this, and what are these resources?

To begin with, a Christian understanding of life calls attention to the finitude that in part defines us as human. The moral and intellectual im-

19. Huntington, *The Clash of Civilizations,* p. 321.

plications of this conviction are obvious. If we live out our lives always aware of our finitude, we should welcome occasions to expand our horizons in encounters with others who are different from ourselves. As Christians we are called to the practice of an intellectual humility that comes with a healthy awareness of our limits, listening to perspectives other than our own, and doing so patiently, charitably, and self-critically. This does not mean that we should lack Christian conviction, or that we should be reluctant to declaim passionately on behalf of the truth of the gospel. After all, those who have not yet acknowledged Christ as Lord are as human as we are, limited by nature, and thus in principle ought to be willing to hear us describe the "reason for the hope within us."

Just as for human finitude, our belief in the fallen state of humankind and the noetic effects of sin works in two directions. Not only are our hearts and minds in need of redemption, but we believe that all people stand in need of the transforming grace of God. As we encounter those who disagree with us, we should respond with gentleness, as Peter's epistle describes, aware of how deeply rooted are our sinful tendencies toward prideful disdain of those who are unlike us.

Our willingness to treat others respectfully, of course, is grounded in a third Christian theological conviction. We profess the worth of every human person as created by God, loved by God, and capable of being redeemed by God's grace for eternal fellowship with him. Because Christ commands us to "love our neighbor as ourselves," we must engage in the diligent discipleship that produces evidence of the fruit of the Spirit in our lives as we mature in the faith. As the Holy Spirit works in our lives, it becomes possible for us to acknowledge the worth of others, to love them, and to long prayerfully for their own redemption in Christ. It is God's love that creates us, it is Christ's love that redeems us, it is through the work of the Spirit that we accept one another as brothers and sisters in Christ, and it is our love for the world around us that compels us to be faithful in reaching out to others in Christ's name. And if this kind of love shapes our lives, we will practice Christian hospitality. Indeed, one way of understanding Christian hospitality is as a concrete practice showing our commitment to love of neighbor.

Human finitude, our predilection to sin, the unconditional love of others, and the practice of Christian hospitality all provide theological resources that affect the way Christians should relate to others in a multicivilizational world. Without relativizing the faith, they give us reason to engage others constructively. They help us avoid the twin poles that Tillich rightly critiques: radical rejection of and radical adaptation to culture. They help us negotiate a way, admittedly fraught with difficulty, between reactionary and accommodationist, between legalist and libertarian, between self-certain smugness and laissez-faire relativism. They help us remain committed to missionary practices grounded in the Great Commission, while avoiding the cultural imperialism that too often has gone hand-in-hand with our evangelizing efforts.

The Challenge for Christian Higher Education in a Multicivilizational World

Christian colleges and universities face challenges on many fronts in trying to stay true to their missions as Christian institutions. George Marsden has compellingly described many of these challenges in his seminal book on higher education, *The Soul of the American University.* In this remarkable *tour de force,* he offers a very sensitizing history of the whole development of American higher education from Harvard in 1636 to the present. Among other things, he relates how the decline of a pervasive Christian culture has resulted in a tendency toward secularization in American higher education. The challenges Marsden identifies remain with us. To them, alas, we must add the challenge of remaining faithfully Christian in a multicivilizational world. What, then, of the role of Christian higher education? How do the resources outlined above, in light of the challenges Huntington identifies, bear on Christian liberal arts education? As a beginning, among the lessons to be learned by Western Christian higher education from the pressing challenges Huntington presents are:

The Value of Studying Western Civilization

This may constitute a counterintuitive proposal, for perhaps it seems we should study Western civilization less rather than more in a truly multicivilizational world. Nevertheless, I submit that our institutions must attend to serious study of Western civilization, including the great philosophers from ancient Greece to the present. Therein are significant ideas, alternatives, and values encountered that prepare students to think

171

carefully and with integrity about life's important values. Therein students develop the resources to think critically, both about the Western tradition and alternatives to it. Therein the skill of creative, imaginative reflection that regards things deeply and envisions possibilities yet to be realized is cultivated.

Former United Nations General Assembly President Charles Malik was an evangelical Orthodox Christian from Lebanon. Several years ago he complained of the anti-intellectualism prevalent among evangelicals. He recommended that students spend a year studying Plato's *Republic,* or two years Aristotle's *Ethics,* or three years Augustine's *City of God.* This, he said, must be done to be a more effective witness to Christ.

The Need for Significant Attention to Church History

The study of secular history gives valuable lessons for tomorrow's leaders. However, the study of church history, perhaps more than any other subject, will give students a grasp of the development of Christian thought from ancient times, through the early settlement of the American frontier until today. It will engender understanding of why Christian doctrine is important, the cultural and intellectual currents to which it often was a clarifying response, and the alternatives to orthodox belief and practice that Christians have countenanced and rejected in centuries past. As with study of Western civilization's great texts, careful attention to church history nurtures both sympathetic understanding and self-criticism. The warning that those who fail to learn from history must repeat it is valid here.

The Legitimate Christian Prejudice of the Christian College

Tertullian's question, "What does Jerusalem have to do with Athens?" reminds us that there is a distinct Christian tradition separate from Western secular culture. Compromising the faith, by either wholesale adaptation or disengaged preservation, will doom Christian higher education to either extinction or irrelevancy. Christian education must always proceed in creative and self-critical engagement with the wider culture, but it must do so without yielding firm commitment to Jesus Christ as Lord. It was a sad experience for me to attend the baccalaureate service of a historically Christian college. Christ was intentionally left out of the hymns, the prayers, the Scripture, and the sermon. Apparently in trying not to offend anyone, it was thought wise to exclude the mention of Christ. If Christian colleges are ashamed of a bold faith in Christ, then I see no purpose in calling them Christian.

The Imperative Commitment to Relate to Other Cultures

In higher education, Christians must be sensitive to young men and women from other cultures and the religions they bring with them. This does not mean that we should also deny our own faith. A conversion theology of the cross must be communicated. A school that is not concerned about bringing all students, foreign and domestic, to a saving knowledge of Jesus Christ forfeits the right to call itself a Christian school. The problem in witnessing to overseas cultures is the same as that of the perception of the West by other civilizations. If our own portrayal of the faith is relativistic, secular, and morally bankrupt, then the faith cannot be communicated. This challenge is not only to the college or university, but to the church.

The Radical Reformation of the Church

The church needs to be radically renewed or else it too will become a dead institution that lives by trust funds and not by faith. The state of spirituality on the college campus is only a reflection of the spirituality of the churches from which our students come. If their faith is superficial, likely the Sunday School and church from which they come was superficial or legalistic. Not only must the Christian faith minister to culture within cultural means, it must also be a prophetic voice against the sin and excesses of depraved and godless culture. The college and university could have a unique role in reforming the church, if students gain a new vision of the crucified and risen Christ in their lives and that of their peers and faculty and administrators.

The Continuing Relevance of Worldwide Mission

What does this clash of civilizations mean for the modern missionary movement? Is it doomed to mere dialogue with other religions? Must we sacrifice our faith at the shores of another civilization? On the contrary, a new kind of servant leader is called for. A new kind of missionary and mission is called for — less arrogant, less imperialistic, less controlled by finances, and more controlled by mutual respect, partnership, sharing, and equal say in finances. The call of Christ is for compassion and dialogue. But it is more than that. It is a vision of the kingdom of God that one day will encompass all of humanity when all the nations of the world will gather at the throne of God and when the "kingdom of the world has become the kingdom of our Lord and of his Christ, and he shall reign for ever and ever" (Rev. 11:15). This is the sustaining vision for every generation of Christians in its clash with the kingdoms and powers of this world. Indeed, we should not fear the clash of civilizations because, contrary to Huntington, we see the kingdom of God as encompassing all of humanity, and all civilizations, not just the West. Christian colleges and universities have a continuing role to play in creating the conditions within which this new kind of missionary and mission may serve God's kingdom.

Christian Higher Education's Prospects for Flourishing in a Multicivilizational World

With such significant challenges, is there any hope on the horizon? As Christians our answer is of course a resounding "Yes!" The Christian college or university more than ever in the twenty-first century can be a beacon of hope in a helpless world. Indeed, as Christian educators, we must be a people of hope, a people whose hope is grounded in the crucified and risen Lord Jesus Christ who is the beginning and end of history. What is the future of Christian higher education in the twenty-first century? I think the best and brightest days are ahead of us. By no means is this the time for pessimism. If our churches open themselves up to renewal, then students and faculty will also be renewed. Conversely, if there is a renewal of spirituality and deep conversion on our campuses, it may be that a new awakening will be ignited from the faculty and students of our colleges. Let us go into the twenty-first century with hope and joy, knowing that "He who began a good work in you will bring it to completion" (Phil. 1:6).

QUESTIONS FOR REFLECTION AND DISCUSSION

1. Huntington describes Christianity as "historically the single most important characteristic of Western civilization," but also offers an account detailing the decline of Western influence in the world. This might suggest the decline of Christian influence in the world, except as Lotz notes, Western civilization is not the only locus of Christianity. Indeed, Huntington himself notes the explosive growth of Christianity in China, Korea, and Latin America, among other places. How should the shifting locus of world Christianity shape American Christian higher education?

2. Lotz asks whether "understanding and cooperation among the political, spiritual, and intellectual leaders of the world's major civilizations" is possible. What Christian doctrines and practices should inform a response to this question? How could the curriculum of Christian colleges and universities introduce students to these resources?

3. In response to the challenges of relating to a multicivilizational world, Lotz argues that Christian higher education should emphasize the serious study of Western civilization, a clear sense of church history, and unyielding witness to Jesus as Lord, while demonstrating a sensitive understanding of other religions. Does the counsel Lotz offers to Christian educators make sense in a multicivilizational context? Why or why not?

4. In a section of his book entitled "La Revanche de Dieu," Huntington points out that while through the mid-twentieth century "intellectual elites generally assumed that economic and social modernization was leading to the withering away of religion . . . the second half of the twentieth century proved these hopes and fears unfounded" (p. 94). How might this surprising turn-about provide renewed credibility for the project of Christian higher education in America?

Contributors

Anthony Campolo is professor emeritus of sociology at Eastern University in St. Davids, Pennsylvania. An ordained Baptist minister and well-known activist and writer, Campolo is the founding director of the Evangelical Association for the Promotion of Education (EAPE), a ministry that seeks Christian transformation of individual lives and whole neighborhoods, mobilizing people to live sacrificially the whole gospel of Jesus Christ. He has made appearances on several national media programs, and is the author of numerous books addressing political and social issues from a Christian perspective.

Joel A. Carpenter is the provost of Calvin College, a post he has held since 1996. He is the former director of the Religion Program at Pew Charitable Trusts, a position he assumed after a dozen years in teaching posts at Calvin College, Trinity College (Illinois), and Wheaton College. Carpenter is the author of the award-winning study, *Revive Us Again: The Reawakening of American Fundamentalism.* His latest work, co-edited with Lamin Sanneh, is *The Changing Face of Christianity: Africa, the West, and the World.*

C. Stephen Evans is University Professor of Philosophy and Humanities at Baylor University. Prior to coming to Baylor, Evans served in teaching posts at Wheaton College, St. Olaf College, where he was Curator of the Howard and Edna Hong Kierkegaard Library, and Calvin

College, where he served as Dean for Research and Scholarship. His published work includes over a dozen books, among which are *Faith Beyond Reason, The Historical Christ and the Jesus of Faith: The Incarnational Narrative as History,* and *Passionate Reason: Making Sense of Kierkegaard's* Philosophical Fragments.

Nathan O. Hatch, Andrew V. Tackes Professor of History, became Notre Dame's provost in 1996. Appointed to the Tackes Chair in 1999 and a member of the faculty since 1975, Hatch regularly is cited as one of the most influential scholars in the study of the history of religion in America. His award-winning book, *The Democratization of American Christianity,* was called by Professor Gordon Wood of Brown University "the best book on religion in the early Republic that has ever been written," and was chosen in a survey of two thousand historians and sociologists as one of the two most important books written on the study of American religion.

Arthur F. Holmes taught philosophy at Wheaton College until his retirement in 1994. During a distinguished tenure of over forty years at Wheaton, he actively promoted the integration of faith and learning among his colleagues and students, and is widely recognized for his efforts in revitalizing Christian involvement in professional philosophy. Author or editor of many books, including most recently *Building the Christian Academy,* Holmes continues service to Christian higher education not only through his writing, but as a frequent lecturer and board member of the Institute for Advanced Christian Studies (IFACS).

Richard T. Hughes, Distinguished Professor of Religion at Pepperdine University, also directs Pepperdine's Center for Faith and Learning. A scholar and classroom teacher for over thirty years, Hughes has published extensively in American religious history and the relation between Christianity and American higher education. His several edited or authored books include *Illusions of Innocence: Protestant Primitivism in America, 1630-1857; Reviving the Ancient Faith: The Story of Churches of Christ in America; Models for Christian Higher Education: Strategies for Success in the Twenty-First Century,* and *How Christian Faith Can Sustain the Life of the Mind.*

177

Denton Lotz serves as General Secretary of the Baptist World Alliance, a fellowship uniting over two hundred Baptist conventions and unions comprising a community of over one hundred million Baptists worldwide. In this role, he is responsible for overseeing the Baptist World Alliance's efforts to provide fellowship, meet human need, lead in evangelism, and work for justice around the world. Lotz serves as the official representative of the Baptist World Alliance to meetings of Baptist bodies and other Christian groups, various world governments, and nongovernmental organizations, and in that role travels, lectures, and preaches extensively.

Martin E. Marty is the Fairfax M. Cone Distinguished Service Professor Emeritus at the University of Chicago Divinity School, where he taught for thirty-five years and where he founded the Martin Marty Center to promote "public religion" endeavors. He writes the "M.E.M.O" column for the biweekly *Christian Century,* on whose staff he has served since 1956, and is well known for his dozens of scholarly works on religion and public life, including ongoing work as editor of a multivolume series on fundamentalism, *The Fundamentalism Project.*

Parker J. Palmer is a writer, teacher, and activist interested in education, community, leadership, spirituality, and social change. His work spans a wide range of institutions, including universities, public schools, community organizations, religious institutions, corporations, and foundations. Presently serving as Senior Associate of the American Association of Higher Education, Palmer's work has been featured by *The New York Times, The Chronicle of Higher Education,* and *The Christian Century,* among others.